HIS POWER IS AMONG US:
THE STORY OF A
HEALING MINISTRY

HIS POWER IS AMONG US:
THE STORY OF A
HEALING MINISTRY

Compiled and Edited by Patricia A.Kelly, Ph.D.

Published by:
Queenship Publishing
P.O. Box 42028
Santa Barbara, CA 93140-2028

Printed in the United States of America

In Prayerful Dedication to Our Lady of La Salette, Our Mother, Our Reconciler

Our Lady of La Salette
intercede for us

FOREWORD

Her head was buried in her hands, her elbows rested on her knees. In the posture of bent grief, the beautiful lady wept. And when she stood, the tears continued to rain down, disappearing in the radiance that suffused her.

The darkness of her sorrowing attitude was softened by the light of her promise in this apparition of Our Lady, revealed to two shepherd children on a mountaintop in La Salette, France on Sept. 19, 1846. She appeared as the tender and compassionate mother weeping for her children. She appeared as the bearer of good news, mediating mother, reconciler, before God, of the people of her Son.

Mary's tears of love continue to inform and to transform the mission of the priests and brothers of the La Salette Order, who in 1992 celebrated the centenary of their coming to America.

Tears are the touchstones of our deepest emotions, our psychological and physical pain. They are also a purging prelude to healing.

Perhaps, then, it is part of the "grace called La Salette," that — as the work of the Order extended in this land to a century's close — certain of its missionaries would hear and heed the call to a healing ministry. One such priest is Rev. Albert A. Fredette, whose path, during the forty years since his ordination, has crisscrossed the United States and wound through the Philippines.

From Buckman, Minnesota, to Havelock, North Carolina, to Cape Cod, Massachusetts, to Manila, Father Fredette has made the message known. He has preached in churches where the pews have been packed and the suffering have streamed in from the street, queuing up to be prayed over for healing.

He has brought his ministry to far more private settings as well, asking the Father for blessings on homes and generations of family who gather there, in their kitchens, in their living rooms, celebrating the Eucharist at the table where they share their daily meals.

He has taught to drop-in crowds in the open-air settings of flea markets, and he has instructed the self-selected audiences of seminars and workshops.

He has offered prayer for the sick and the dying in the somber confines of hospital rooms.

He has conducted planned healing services by invitation, in places where his parishioners have been his congregation.

He has ministered with no notice and without formality to passing strangers who are in need.

Wherever his journey of that hour, that day, that week, that month or those months may end, it has brought good news to the children of God who hunger for it. It has brought validation to many that the healing power of Mary's Son is still among us.

If the journey of Fr. Fredette's ministry were to have a signature, it would be simplicity. Remember that Our Lady of La Salette appeared to lowly shepherd children, and what she said was straightforward and unadorned. So, too, the message of this book.

We will learn how Father Fredette became a channel for Christ's healing. We will learn how we can reach for healing. We will learn how we can be healers for others, in our contemporary families, in our ancestry, in our workplaces, in the widest context of the community at large.

And the lessons are gently taught by a man of quiet word, who shares spiritual concepts so simple we are sorely tempted to underestimate the measure of their truth, and the magnitude of their power.

It is Father Fredette's voice you will hear most often in prayer, in lesson, in explanation. But there are other voices as well, providing thanksgiving and praise along the way, serving as signposts that the journey of his ministry is one blessed and well spent.

They form a kind of hallelujah chorus — these stories of men, women and children willing and very much wanting to witness to the compassionate, healing power of Jesus Christ.

They are people of tears, and they are children of La Salette. The figure of Our Lady bowed in sorrow on that mountaintop in France is an icon that images the transfiguration of their lives.

"Our Lady of La Salette asks nothing for herself... She holds the secret all people want to learn. She knows better than poets or statesmen, better than a loving sister or anyone in the world, how tears can be turned into joy."[1]

—Patricia A. Kelly, Ph.D.
Chesapeake Beach, Maryland 1993

x

A Reconciler's Prayer
to Our Lady of La Salette

Let your Tears of Love bid us come, children do not be afraid!
Let your Tears of Love intercede, help us find our way.
As you stand beneath the Cross of Christ,
Mary, reconcile us in His Light.

Let your Tears of Love shelter us from the stormy wind and rain.
Let your Tears of Love calm our fears, every hurt, and our pain.
Stay with us and take us by the hand,
Mary, be our refuge in this land.

Let your Tears of Love change our hearts,
lead us back into the fold.
Let your Tears of Love be our Hope on our journey home.
Pray for us who build the Kingdom,
As we wait for that Great Day to come.

Let your Tears of Love bring a new Life in a world of little faith.
Let your Tears of Love comfort us when we see your face,
Mary, when we see your face, your face.

Our Lady of La Salette, Reconciler of sinners,
Pray for us who have recourse to you.

The La Salette Crucifix

This is a unique Cross of reconciliation. It was the most luminous and brilliant part of the Apparition of Our Lady at La Salette in France in 1846. On the left side of the Cross is the pincers and on the right side, the hammer. The hammer represents our sins and our unforgiveness in life, used to nail Jesus to the Cross. The pincers, the instrument used to pull the nails from the hands and feet of Jesus on the Cross of our salvation, represent our forgiveness, sorrow and repentance for our sins. Thus the La Salette Cross is called the Cross of Reconciliation and the title given to Our Blessed Mother at La Salette is "Our Lady of La Salette, Reconciler of sinners." This crucifix is the only one of its kind in the world and in the history of mankind.

COMMENTARY

My friendship with Fr. Al spans nearly two decades. The common thread running through both of our lives is a firm belief in the healing love of Jesus Christ to restore brokenness of body, mind and spirit. Throughout the many years of our friendship, I have seen Fr. Al consistently acknowledge God's power to heal physical and emotional sickness. His story underscores the victory of the cross of Jesus Christ and the message of Our Lady of La Salette.

My first memories of Fr. Al occurred when his adventures in the ministry took a surprising turn with the simple step of making a spiritual retreat at Mt. Augustine Retreat Center in Staten Island, NY, in August 1975. At that time Fr. Al was assigned to St. Vincent Medical Center in Toledo, Ohio as supervisor of clinical pastoral education.

Several times each year a retreat team, consisting of Sr. Jeanne Hill, and Frs. Francis MacNutt and Paul Schaaf and me, customarily presented teachings on the gift of Christian healing. Fr. MacNutt commented on the large number of health care professionals in attendance at the August gathering and suggested they might want to meet in a separate group to discuss common interests.

Dr. Joe Hempsey, an osteopathic physician, described the scene: "Sr. Nadia, Rick and I arrived early. We decided to leave a chair at the head of the table open. Soon others came to join us until we had twenty-two doctors, nurses, psychologists, counselors, dentists, priests and nuns. We all realized something unusual was happening. We began to pray together to see what God was doing. We agreed that whoever came to sit at the head chair would be in charge of whatever this event was. When Fr. Al Fredette entered the room, he was startled when the only vacant chair was at the head of the table. We were silent, but as soon as he sat down, we all pointed laughingly and said, 'You're in charge.'"

It soon became apparent that the Holy Spirit had placed the stamp of approval on the right person. The group expressed an interest in forming an organization of health care professionals who practice Christian healing. Fr. Al carried the concept of the meeting back to Toledo, Ohio, where he utilized St. Vincent Hospital's office facilities to bring to birth the Association of Christian Therapists. It is a tribute to Fr. Al's organizational skills that ACT continues to touch the lives of thousands of persons throughout the world.

Our paths have crossed many times since then and I am always impressed with Fr. Al's enthusiasm for the Gospel message. Even in the face of personal suffering and sorrow, his faith remains planted in the truth of God's love for His people.

His Power Is Among Us: The Story of a Healing Ministry contains the wisdom gleaned from Fr. Al's personal and ministerial experiences throughout 40 years of priesthood. He demonstrates the blend of medicine and prayer by sharing anecdotes covering a wide range of subjects. Interspersed throughout the book are prayers which the reader can adapt to meet individual needs.

The charism of Our Lady of La Salette shines through his writings, especially in the understanding of reconciliation and forgiveness. Fr. Al's spiritual pilgrimage is reminiscent of the injunction, *"Go not where the road may lead, go instead where there is no path and leave a trail."* Many will find his book inspirational and challenging for their own journey toward wholeness and holiness.

— Barbara Shlemon Ryan
President, Be-Loved Ministry,
Brea, California, January, 1994

ACKNOWLEDGMENTS

We are especially indebted to Jim Gibbons, Lilly E. O'Brien, Mary Robinson, Francesca Ricco, Susan and Joseph B. Fredette, Paul and Dot Seguin and Bertha Seguin for their volunteered assistance in transcription; to Richard E. Kelly for his technical support; and to the following persons who witnessed to the compassionate healing power of Jesus in thanksgiving and so that others might believe: Marian J. Desrosiers, Kim and Lynn Francis, Todd Houghton, Dr. Michael Vigorito, Viola Lynch, "Nathaniel's Mother," Renee Gall, Joy Chamberlain and Helen and Dave Logan.

INTRODUCTION

The tears of Our Lady of La Salette reflect the sorrowing solicitude of the Heavenly Mother. They beckon us to reconciliation — without which there can be no healing.

Our tears are mute expressions of our brokenness, our desire for wholeness and holiness and our capacity to be reconcilers and conduits of Christ's healing power for others.

Nothing is so quietly eloquent as silent tears. Nothing is quite so capable of touching the human heart to win it. Tears are the language of suffering humanity, a language that is always heard and understood. Tears are extensions of the anguished soul.

I believe all of us at times have felt that mere words could not contain the meaning of our sorrow, that tears and only tears could express it to hearts that could know our hearts.

I remember, as a boy one day during the summer, a sudden storm came upon us as we were playing outside, and we were called indoors for shelter. It was when I looked out the window eagerly awaiting the end of the rainfall, that I first realized both the similarities and the differences between a simple drop of water and a human tear shed in pain, or in happiness. As I watched the droplet glide slowly down the pane, spending itself and finally disappearing, I saw it was a prism for both the sparkling beauty of nature renewing and the darker shadows of the storm.

In the tear that we cry, as in the raindrop, are contained and reflected the human suffering and joys that make up the story of the soul.

The human tear perhaps resembles more the water of the ocean than the rainfall, because it also contains the element of salt. The salt reminds us of the sometimes bitter reality of human existence when tears are spilled in futility, without growth, in unredemptive suffering, in the passions of unbridled anger, hatred, self-pity.

Remember that from the Valley of Bethany where Jesus raised Lazarus, he could see in the distance the Jordan River, a tranquilly flowing and productive water bringing fertility to the area. But this same river flows into the Dead Sea, where there is no life, no growth, only heavy deposits of salt and barren banks. Here life is turned to death.

When Jesus left Bethany, He went away from the Jordan, and He walked up the mountain called Dominus Flevet, where He could see the Jerusalem which rejected him. Yet, beyond Jerusalem, He could also see the life-giving Mediterranean. Jesus wept for Lazarus in the Valley of Bethany. He wept on the mountain. In one instance new life followed — Lazarus was raised from the dead. In the other, death followed. Jerusalem was destroyed.

From the tears of Jesus for His friend we learn we should not weep alone and in self-absorption, but that our love and our sorrow, our compassion and our concern must be shared. As Jesus cried for Lazarus, the crowds said, "See how much He loved him."

The Lord not only wants us to be healed, He calls us to be healers of others in His name, to go beyond ourselves. He calls us forth to help take the bitter sting, the salt, from the tears that flow in our presence: so that they will assume meaning, and purpose, and be fruitful for those shedding them; and be fruitful for us as we humbly recognize ourselves as channels of the healing love of Jesus.

"You will know my disciples by the love they have for each other," Jesus said.

This book is as much about healing others through Christ, as it is about seeking healing for ourselves. The concepts are co-dependent.

We can all rise on the stepping stones of our own selves to higher things, giving praise and glory to God because we care enough to love our brothers and sisters in the family of the children of God. We can help the grieving, the hurting, the afflicted find comfort in the constant loving healer, Jesus Christ. Through the witness of our compassion is revealed His love — the love that transforms darkness and death into a wellspring of light and life.

Brokenness, of course, is a precondition for healing. When Jesus says, "What do you want?", we say, "To be healed, to be reconciled." Touched by His healing power, we experience the healing of our own bodies, minds, souls and emotions.

We also discover, however, that He says, "Go and do likewise." As we assent to heal one another, care for one another, Jesus assents to heal us, care for us. As Dr. Nassif J. Cannon Jr., a physician, points out:

"Genuine healing is not simply a repair process... Genuine healing transcends... to include deep integration of body, mind and spirit... There are priorities in healing. God's priorities may not be ours. Perhaps His highest priority is the healing of the soul, then the mind, then the body."[1]

The message of our beautiful Lady of La Salette, the Reconciler, given 146 years ago, is a message for the healing of the soul — a message which speaks compellingly to us today:

She asks that we convert our hearts and our attitudes from worldliness and attachment to the material to a more divine spirit of forgiveness and love.

She asks that we renew commitment to daily prayer.

She asks that we give honor, respect and obedience to God and reverence to the name of Jesus.

She asks that we remain faithful to God's laws and the laws of the Church.

Remember her tears. They are the tears of maternal care and solicitude, of tenderness and concern for her children. May they remain a sign for us on our healing journeys. May they keep us steadfast and resolved to yearn and reach for reconciliation, to become reconcilers ourselves, in our families, in our workplaces, in our worlds — however far they may extend.

—Rev. Albert A. Fredette, M.S.,
Order of Our Lady of La Salette,
the Shrine of Our Lady of La Salette,
Attleboro, Massachusetts, 1993

AUTHORS' NOTE: Although "redemptive suffering" is not discussed in detail in this work, we recognize that every person is born in human brokenness and, as such, is subject to pain, distress, tensions and a variety of sufferings including illnesses — spiritual, emotional or physical — all of which can be "redemptive" when united to the Passion and Cross of Jesus Christ. As members of the Mystical Body of Christ, we are called to participate and be part of both His death and resurrection, thus witnessing to His Power and Glory. Consequently there is always a presence on earth of both the suffering side and the Resurrection side of the Cross.

TABLE OF CONTENTS

THE STORY OF LA SALETTE BRIEFLY TOLD: A STORY OF RECONCILIATION

(The following abbreviated history of the found-
ing of the La Salette missionary order is both di-
rectly excerpted and summarized in paraphrase from
The Missionaries of La Salette, From France to
North America by Donald Paradis, M.S., La Salette
Publications, 1992, and is included with the per-
mission of the author and La Salette Publications).

La Salette is an obscure village buried in the Alps of southeast-
ern France. There on September 19th, 1846, the Blessed Virgin
Mary appeared to two young cowherds, Maximin Giraud, age 11,
and Melanie Mathieu (Calvat), age 14. In the center of a great circle
of light the two children saw a beautiful woman seated upon a stone,
her face buried in her hands. She was weeping. Then the Beautiful
Lady rose and spoke, "Come my children; do not be afraid. I am
here to tell you great news."

Mary's message to the two children of La Salette was the warn-
ing of a mother concerned over her wayward children. She com-
plained: "If my people refuse to submit, I will be forced to let go
the arm of my Son" and more specifically: "Those who drive the
carts cannot swear without using my Son's name... they labor all
day Sunday... "there are none who go to Mass... when they do not
know what to do, they go to Mass just to make fun of religion... ."
She warned: "If the harvest is ruined, it is only on account of yourselves... If you have wheat, you must not sow it. Anything you
sow the vermin will eat... A great famine is coming... " She promised: "If [my people] are converted, rocks and stones will turn into

heaps of wheat, and potatoes will be self-sown in the fields…" She pleaded: "Well, my children, make this known to all my people…"[1]

Mary's apparition at La Salette is a modern-day reminder of an ancient truth: that Mary constantly intercedes for us before God; that she is the Reconciler of Sinners, calling us back to the message and way of her Son, Jesus.

The La Salette Missionaries are founded upon the reconciling message and mission of this Apparition of Mary. Their congregation numbers about 1,000 priests and brothers serving in over twenty countries around the world.

They originally formed as a small community in May of 1852 at the site of the Apparition to minister to the pilgrims, who began flocking there in numbers of 30,000 annually. Their first habitat was a primitive mountain shack, serving as bedroom, community room, dining room, workroom and parlor, "its ill-fitted planks offering a rare view of the starry alpine sky, and its starkness prompting comparison to the stable at Bethlehem…"[2]

In 1892, La Salette emissaries came to America via Quebec, crossing the border into the United States on July 6. Thus, 1992 marks the centennial of their mission in this land.

A PRAYER FOR THE LA SALETTE CENTENARY

This prayer was composed by Fr. Donald Paradis of the Order of Our Lady of La Salette to mark the centennial observance of the congregation's coming to America.

Mother of the Lord, to whom all ages belong, we entrust to your care the centenary celebration of the coming of the La Salette missionaries to this land. By the Spirit's power, oh Mary, you gave birth to the flesh and history to our world's peace and reconciliation. Speak anew, a challenging call to bring forth a new creation in Christ Jesus. Bearer of Good News, your apparition reminds us that every human reality is bathed in Gospel light. Rekindle the compelling vision that reveals grace at work in the encounters and events of our everyday life. Beautiful Lady, you entrusted your message to the hearts and lips of simple shepherd children. Be with us in a continuing conversation as we recall the story of our congregation's first century as a sign and servant of reconciliation in America. Radiant Queen, the gift you gave from the mountaintop presses on now to its fulfillment. Give our spirits courage before our summoning future, and keep our grateful hearts ever faithful to your message and your tears. AMEN

Chapter 1

HIS POWER IS AMONG US: HOW DO WE KNOW?

As I went from parish to parish, hundreds of parishes over the forty years of my priesthood, I thought that people were hungry for the word of God, and I was delighted. But I found that people were not just hungry, they were starved. We are starved for the word of God, and that word is liberation and freedom.

When we want to see what the Lord did when He came on earth, and when we want to see all the healings, we turn to Mark. Every time we turn another page, there is a new kind of healing. And we say, isn't that amazing? There is every kind of healing in every kind of way because the Lord respected the medical knowledge of His time, so He used minerals, He used oil, spittle, water, He used all the things known at the time to be medicinally beneficial and purifying.

We might say, well that was then, but this is now. His healing presence was there, then, and it is present just as surely here and now.

When He was on earth, walking those dusty streets of Jerusalem or sitting by that well at noon talking to this "terrible" woman of Samaria, He was healing. The perspective Jesus had on that woman was different. He could see what was within her and what she needed most. Instead of condemning her, judging her, He saw that she needed the wellspring of life-giving warmth, and that was what He brought her.

Think of that poor woman. She was abandoned by her own people, was missing out on all the good news of her village. When she came at noon, generally there was nobody there at the well because of the heat. All the other women came early in the morning when it was cool. But this day there was a man there, and he was Jewish. Her people had nothing to do with the Jewish people. So what was he doing here? This was the first time she had even seen a Jewish person, because in those days if you went from Jerusalem to Galilee, you came in the middle of that trek to Samaria. And the Jews would go up and around Samaria because no one would put his foot on the soil of these "awful" people. When Jesus came, He confronted the problem of prejudice squarely, smack in the middle of Samaria, right up to that well.

It went something like this: "How come you are speaking to me, I am Samaritan, you are Jewish,"? she asked. We hate each other, we don't communicate."

"Well, He said, "How about you giving me a drink of water?"

"Me, a Samaritan, give you a Jew some water?"

He said, "If you knew who you were talking to, you would ask me for a drink of water."

She does not understand His language at all. She was talking buckets, He was talking about life-giving waters from within.

And then when He reveals to her her own history, that she did not have a husband, but five men with whom she had lived, one at a time. He did not tell it in a condemning fashion. That was always the difference between the way the Lord spoke with people and the way the Pharisees operated, creating laws and burdens. The Lord came to deliver us from such oppression, and so He spoke to her of living waters.

"Ah, she thought, this must be a great prophet," and she went back to her village renewed. She had found something new, a relationship with someone she was supposed to detest. And she found He was loving of her. He could penetrate the externals, get by all

2

those stories about her and see in her heart. She was thirsty. He brought her yearnings forward to light, so she could value herself as a daughter of the Lord — Yahweh.

We, Too, Are Called

So we consider such stories, and as we read them in the Gospels, we are amazed. We see that no matter where the Lord walked, His presence made a difference. And so today we, too, are called to make a difference, to follow Christ and become like Him. We need to make a difference. We cannot be just mediocre. We need to become aware within ourselves of the spirit of Christ. We need to walk in that Grace. And as we do, with the working of the Spirit within us, we become inspired. We begin to have energies and dedication and commitment at a level we never before experienced.

We begin to do things beyond our abilities. And when we do, we should turn around and give thanks, for the Lord has passed. He has left His presence with us which transforms us into the children of God.

We begin to know who we are. And that knowledge speaks to our hearts. We can respond to it. Do we still say, "Oh, yes, okay, when the Lord walked those streets, there were miracles and healings, one after another, but where is He today? What kind of marvelous things is He doing today among the people of God?"

In the pages to come, I will share with you stories of the healings through God I have encountered in my ministry. Some of those stories will be in my words; others will be recounted by those who experienced the healings.

And we will explore in detail the concept of healing ministry. But, in capsule form, the healing ministry is this: If you have an illness, spiritually, emotionally, physically — that is a lack of wholeness, and we call that evil. It is not good. So when we pray, as a community of faith, over that person in need of healing, what we are doing is calling upon this person through us the compassionate, gentle healing power of Jesus Christ. We are asking that the Lord Himself in His perfect humanity come and meet the needs of this person seeking help. We are asking the Lord to borrow from His perfect humanity that which is lacking in the humanity of that person in need of healing. If there is more love coming from the community of faith than the existing evil, then the compassionate love of Jesus overpowers the evil, and healing occurs. That is how it works.

Healing is the work of God. There is no magic in God's healing of the spirit, the mind and the body. All we are called to do is minister His love and power to the people who ask for it. We know He called us: "Come, follow me." As healing ministers, we need to recall John: 14:12. Jesus said, "He who believes in me will also do the works that I do, and greater works than these will He do." And so we need to step out in the boldness of Christ into the settings, the family, the work and play places, the community and be healers to our world.

Raising Our Community Consciousness

This concept of a community of faith is integral to the process of healing and to the development of ourselves as healing persons. There is an image I summon when I pray. Think of this: Every Christian is a member of the Mystical Body of Christ. So I envision the whole world of Christians coming together when I pray. Remember, we are never alone in prayer. We could go to China, for instance, and ask every Christian there the following question: "Would you agree with me that we are going to pray for our sister or our brother who is in need of healing?" Of course, every Christian everywhere would say, "Yes, we will do it."

But since we cannot physically go forth to individually ask for this, then we need to be united in spirit, embracing in our prayer all the members of the Mystical Body of Christ. In that way we are totally before the Father in the petition that we raise up to Him.

With such a vision we have such strength, and our hope should be enkindled and deepened, knowing that every Christian on earth will agree with us and pray for our brethren in need.

There is a distinction that needs to be made and maintained between healing through a community of faith and so-termed "faith-healing." Faith healing, the television variety, places the burden of faith on the person petitioning for help. So if the person is not healed, then he is blamed for not having sufficient faith. That is not the Lord's way, leaving a person more broken after praying than before. This "faith-healing" is deceptive, and deception is the work of the devil.

Where two or three gather in the Lord's name, agree upon asking the Father for what you want, and believe you have it. Can you imagine bringing that kind of power into your family? Can you imagine brothers and sisters, parents and children all in unison about what is good for one another, praying that it might happen? Well, it will happen, and we will explore this subject further when we examine how to restore peace to families through prayer. The community of faith can exist within the family as well as in our extended social settings.

The Healing Power of Community Prayer

When I worked at St. Vincent's Medical Center in Toledo, Ohio, there was a minister who was a patient there. His doctor stopped by and told me of him, indicating that he was a Lutheran pastor, and he had three months to live, cancer having been diagnosed. The physician asked me to see him. When I visited the room, the pastor asked if I could come to his church on a Sunday to show a film, "The Power of Healing Prayer" and speak to his congregation. I did that, and after the presentation, I said, "Let us make a prayer to the Lord, right now, that your pastor will be restored to the fullness of health." The pastor had been doing ministry to shut-ins.

I said, "Where two or more are gathered in his name, that is a community of faith. So agree on what you want, no dissension, ask the Father for anything, and make, like St. Paul says, petitions filled with gratitude."

They agreed that they wanted complete restoration of health for him. I led a prayer asking that the compassionate healing power of Christ touch every cell in his body. Then I left. A little later I got another call saying the pastor wanted to see me again. He said, "You know, it is not in the Lutheran tradition to have blessed oil, and I know it is the Catholic tradition. I believed that for twenty years, but now I wonder if you would come to a service, and we will have the blessing of the oil, and to show my people I believe in it, I will be the first one to be blessed with it. And then we will invite them all to come and be blessed and be prayed over."

That evening we went to a meeting of the elders of that church, and the pastor's physician was there. The doctor asked the pastor, "Is it okay for me to share with Father Al and the elders what has happened to you"? The pastor smiled broadly and said, "Yes."

The doctor said, "I took new tests of my patient. There is no cancer. This is a miracle. I had never said anything like that. But this is a miracle."

Then we went to the church, and the pastor warned me that there might not be many people. Well, the church was full, and we blessed the people with the oil, and many were healed. The pastor lived nine more years to serve God, having been restored to full health for that period, after his community asked for that healing from Jesus.

My Hand, Your Hand, Their Hand, His Hand

I have used in my ministry a hand meditation which both helps to bring us in touch with our membership in the community of faith and to increase our awareness that His presence and His power is among us, with us, through us. I invite you to experience it in a group setting:

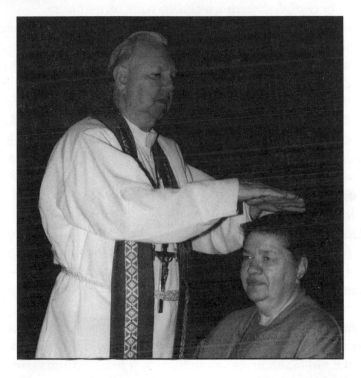

Assume a meditative posture with eyes closed, hands resting in your lap. Tune into your breathing, relax your tension points. Become aware of the air at your fingertips, between your fingers, on the palm of your hand. Experience the fullness, strength, and maturity of your hands. Think of your hands, think of the most unforgettable hand you have known — the hands of your father, your mother, your grandparents. Remember the oldest hands that have rested in your hands. Think of the hands of a newborn child. Think of the incredible beauty, perfection, delicacy in the hands of a child. Once upon a time, your hands were the same size.

Think of all that your hands have done since then. Almost all that you have learned has been through your hands — turning yourself over, crawling and creeping, walking and balancing your-self, washing and bathing, dressing yourself. At one time your greatest accomplishment was tying your own shoes.

Think of all the learning your hands have done and how many activities they have mastered, the things they have made. Remember the day you could write your own name.

Our hands were not just for ourselves, but for others. Recall how often they were given to help another. Remember all the kinds of work they have done, the tiredness and aching they have known, the cold and the heat, the soreness and the bruises. Remember the tears they have wiped away, our own, or another's, the blood they have bled, the healing they have experienced. How much hurt, anger and even violence they have expressed, and how much gentleness, tenderness and love they have given.

Think of how often they have been folded in prayer, both a sign of their powerlessness and their power. Our father and mother guided these hands in the great symbolic language of our hands — the sign of the cross, the striking of our breast, the handshake, the wave of the hand in 'hello' and goodbye."

There is a mystery which we discover in the hand of a woman or the hand of a man whom we love. There are the hands of a doctor, a nurse, an artist, a conductor, a priest, hands which you can never forget.

Now raise your right hand slowly and gently place it over your heart. Press more firmly until your hand picks up the beat of your heart, that most mysterious of all human sounds, one's own heartbeat, a rhythm learned in the womb from the heartbeat of one's mother. Press firmly for a moment and then release your hand and hold it just a fraction from your clothing. Experience the warmth between your hand and your heart. Now lower your hand to your lap very carefully as if it were carrying your heart. For it does. When you extend your hand to another, it is not just bone and skin, it is your heart. A handshake is the real heart transplant.

Think of all the hands that have left their imprint upon you. Fingerprints and hand prints and heart prints that can never be erased. The hand has its own memory. Think of all the places that carry hand prints and all the people who bear your heart print. They are indelible and will last forever.

Now without opening your eyes, extend your hands on either side and find another hand. Do not simply hold it, but explore it and sense the history and mystery of this hand. Let your hand speak to it and let it listen to the other. Try to express your gratitude for this hand outstretched to you in the dark, and then bring your hand back again to your lap. Experience the presence of that hand lingering upon your hand. The afterglow will fade, but the print is there forever.

Whose hand was that? It could have been any hand; it could have been His hand. It was. He has no other hands than ours.

Our Hands Are His Hands

This is such an important and beautiful truth. We need to know that it is not just through the Apostles, not only through the Disciples that Jesus chose to exercise power to heal the sick. They were called first. But through them and through the Church, all of us Christians are called. We are not all called to the same degree, but we are called. As believers we share in the healing power of Jesus through the presence of the Holy Spirit. We need to be open to that. Let us begin our journey through this book with a prayer to our Father, asking for the gift of openness:

Eternal Father, we give You praise, adoration and thanksgiving in all things. We are grateful to You for this opportunity to communicate with one another as your children. You love us because you created us in Your likeness and Your image, and that is good. We ask that You send the gift from the Holy Spirit

to each one of us, the gift of openness, so that our minds and spirit, our emotions, our total self may be open to hear the Word of God, Jesus Christ, and hearing His Word, Your Word, Eternal Father, we may be healed, and we may become healers. We make this prayer through Christ our Lord. AMEN

Chapter 2

HOW DID HE LEAD?
HOW DO WE FOLLOW?

If we as Christians are to continue the mission of Jesus on earth, in the very midst of where we live and work, play and pray, all in His name and through His power, then we need to familiarize ourselves with His ministry. And after we do so, then it is appropriate for us to examine our hearts and minds with the question, "Can, I, too, be a healer, the Lord's instrument, a conduit of his healing power and compassionate love? And, if not, why not? Can I discern what obstacles prevent me from ministering the healing powers of Jesus unto others? Can I overcome those barriers and follow Jesus of Nazareth?"

For Jesus does invite us to share the dominion He has been given over all created things so that we might be His emissaries. We need to be obedient to the Father and in submission to Jesus on this. Think of submission as "sub-mission." The mission is His, and we come like sub-contractors. All of us, no exception, are empowered in differing kind and degree, depending on the talents and gifts received, to do in our times what He did in His.

What, then, was the work of Jesus on earth? He taught, He preached, and He healed. We are told in Matthew 4:23 that Jesus traversed Galilee teaching in the synagogues, preaching the Good News of the Kingdom and healing people of every kind of disease and sickness. The news of Him spread through the whole country of Syria, and people brought Him those suffering all kinds of afflictions — demons, epilepsy, paralysis. And Jesus healed them all, no exceptions. Great crowds followed him to Galilee and the ten towns from Jerusalem and Judea and the land on the other side of the Jordan.

Here we see Jesus healing — physically, emotionally, and, of course, spiritually. Every time He talks about casting out demons, He is talking about the spiritual world and spiritual healing.

We are beings with three main dimensions; one is spirit, one is psychic, one is physical. If there is an imbalance in any one of these areas, disharmony prevails and we become sick. Often when we are unwell spiritually or emotionally, it will manifest itself in the least resistant part of our body.

As evening would come, these beleaguered people of His times, many who had demons, were brought to Jesus, and He ministered to them. His heart filled with pity because they were troubled and helpless, like sheep without a shepherd. He told his Disciples that there was a great harvest, but few workers to gather it. He called them and gave them authority to drive out evil spirits and to heal every affliction.

But that charge was not reserved for Apostles and is not reserved for priests. We are all called as Christians, called with equal urgency. We are also people born into human brokenness. No one among us is perfect, or ever shall be on this earth. We are victims of our own sins and the sins of the world. We are the lonely, the unloved, the rejected. We are prisoners of a culture we did not create and are powerless to change. Does it mean we can refuse to answer the call from Jesus to follow Him?

Paul reminds us that He entrusts the message of reconciliation to us all. No one is exempt from doing God's work. First let us be reconciled; then let us be ministers of reconciliation. As wounded healers, we must reach out to others.

For the Lord does not want anyone to be sick. Never, never once, anywhere in the Gospels, do we find the Lord telling someone who asked for healing to keep his illness, to offer it up to the

Father in heaven, to suffer for a fine place, a plush throne in heaven. Remember that the only thing God promised His Apostles and us, as Christians, was persecution, not illness.

Remember, too, that very few people on earth are chosen by God, Himself, to represent the suffering side of the Cross. I have only met one such person. These people know who they are because they are asked by the Lord to suffer. These people agree to it and joyfully carry their suffering, with such an attitude being a deep form of prayer.

I knew a sister in the pastoral care department of St. Vincent Medical Center in Toledo, Ohio who was called by God to so suffer. One day she was on crutches going up a corridor. She stopped and asked me to pray over her, not to relieve her pain, but help her to bear it. That is true and redemptive suffering. When we do experience trials, we can transform them by joining them to the Lord's agonies so we might enjoy the sunshine side of the Cross. But, I repeat, never did Christ in all the Gospels tell anyone to bear illness and offer it up to the Father. It is not God's will that His children suffer. It is His will that they be healed.

The First Healing, The First Miracle

So much of the Gospels is devoted to healing, reflecting the priority it had for Jesus' mission, dramatizing the terrible need for it among His people. I believe that Jesus' most spectacular healing was His first healing and really His first miracle.

It is commonly held that His first miracle was changing water into wine. No, it was not. The first miracle occurred when, after He had sought out and selected some of his Apostles following the desert experience, He waited for the Sabbath. Then He went to the synagogue in Capernaum, a town in Galilee, with his Apostles, and He opened the Book and impressed His congregation because He taught with great authority. (Luke: 4:31-37).

It was a man possessed by a devil shouting through him, calling out, "Ha, what do you want with us, Jesus of Nazareth? Have you come to destroy us?" And the Lord's response was: "Quiet, now you come out of him." He did not shout, nor make a demonstration. He was quiet, because He had the authority, and He knew who He was. The Gospel tells us that the devil came out of the individual, throwing him down, but not hurting him, and he woke up unto himself. That was the first miracle.

He came, He liberated from what was oppressing, and His first miracle was taking authority over the devil. The people thought, "Who is this? He does not speak like the Scribes or Pharisees, but He commands even the devil, and they listen to Him. Is this a new teaching?" Never before in the history of mankind had it occurred that the devil was dethroned from a person he infested.

Changing the water to wine was a kind of convenience because there was plenty of wine already. But releasing a person from the oppression of the devil, that is really major. This was the Good News of Jesus Christ, son of God, coming to earth to free us. When we think of being liberated from evil spirits, we do not necessarily always refer to the evil spirit as an entity unto itself, as a spirit with a name.

But some evil spirits are of our own making. They can be destructive habits which are not Christian, and they need to be cast out in the name of Jesus. Can that be done today, as it was in Jesus's time? Of course. But you have to humble yourself to ask the Lord. You should not hesitate to invite Him. Ask and you shall receive, seek and you will find, knock at the door of His heart and it will be open to you. As if it is not enough to tell us once, He tells us again and again. It is easy to remember to do this. What are the first letters of "Ask, Seek and Knock"? They are "A" and "S" and "K," and they spell ASK.

Without Christ we can do nothing. Consider the story of Zacchaeus and how Christ's healing presence came to him:

The Story of Zacchaeus: Who Called Whom?

Zacchaeus was a chief tax collector and a wealthy man. (Luke 19:1-10) He heard about Jesus of Nazareth and decided he wanted to meet this man of influence and power who was going to walk through his town of Jericho. That was the first thing, a desire to meet Him. The next step — he invested personally in that meeting, going to the place where there was a crowd already gathered.

Now Zacchaeus was a man small of physical stature, so he pushed his way through the throng to get up front for a better view. No, that was not good enough. So he climbed a sycamore tree to get an unobstructed look.

He decided to invite the Lord into his life because seeing Him and hearing His word, you just decide that. Within his heart, he had the invitation for the Lord already, and what ensued was that the Lord did not wait for him to express it. He invited himself. He said, "Zacchaeus, come down from there because today I must stay at your house."

"How does he know my name?" Zacchaeus thought.

This story contains lessons on the healing process. If we want Jesus to be within ourselves, we have to do something about it. And when we do, He has not even waited for that, but says "I will come and I will be with you." And the Gospel tells us that Zacchaeus receives Jesus with joy.

The healing ministry does not have to be ponderous and heavy and very, very serious with people praying ponderously and heavily and very, very seriously. There is delight in it, and the Lord has a sense of humor. Think of it. Zacchaeus plans all this carefully. He is going to issue an invitation to the Lord, and the Lord just invites Himself!

That is how He speaks to us, and now we have to receive Him with uplifted, expectant faith, giving Him first place in our lives.

How The Lord Healed Me

Zacchaeus rejoiced in experiencing God in his life, and there is no way I, too, can forget the joy His healing presence brought to me. This is what happened:

I used to travel to Windsor, Ontario, Canada where I have two friends in the La Salette Order who took care of a parish there. We decided one Saturday to take time off to pray together. We took the phone off the hook for about an hour and a half. As I sat down I thought, "Al, you have to ask them to pray over you to set you free." That just kept coming to mind. I did not know what it meant.

But I did know that from the time I went into the seminary at the age of 14, I was very very shy, and had been until this day when we prayed. So I asked my friends to pray over me to set me free, and as they laid hands on me, I had a vision deep inside myself:

I was a little boy, before I could walk, sitting there in diapers on the floor of the kitchen of the house in which I was born. The kitchen was streaming with light, and in the background, my parents' room was dark, the shades drawn, my mother sick in bed. I had a top in my hand, the kind you push down and it makes noise, but I could not use the top.

All the time the priests prayed over me, I had this vision, and I could not get rid of it until they stopped praying. Then, I chuckled and said, "Well I have got to tell you what happened to me while you were praying over me." But one of the priests said, "Wait a minute Al, let me tell you what I saw ten minutes before you asked us to pray." And he proceeded to describe in detail my vision.

What was the meaning for me? I later asked my sister if my mother was sick when I was very young. She said, "Oh, yes, she was very sick, so sick that no one could make any noise in the house." Then it made sense. The experience in the vision marked the beginning of my inability to be myself. I could not be a little child making noise. I could not use that top; I could not do what a little child should be permitted to do. I had been scarred as rejected from that moment until the evening those friends prayed over me.

On that evening, after they had prayed, I said Mass and had no time to prepare a homily. But I preached, and several people came to the rectory afterwards and said, "What happened to you, Father Al, that was a great homily!" I did not know what to say, but I think what happened was that I was free enough to be who I am supposed to be. From that time on, I knew that the Lord had entered my life.

The Lord speaks to us in different ways. He speaks to me through the Holy Spirit's gift of discernment, as well as in dreams and visions. For me there were subsequent episodes of healing areas of my life in need of healing.

I remember one dream similar in nature and in time frame to the vision I have recounted, but this time it brought me back to the crib. Can you imagine remembering that?   no way. There I was in the crib, silent, eyes closed, and the sense was that there was no point in my crying because no one would come. In the background, the shades of my parents' room were drawn again, and it was very dark, and my mother was in bed very ill. And in the dream, she got up and came over to me. She was a young woman when I was born, but in this episode she was elderly with gray hair and very sick. She came up to the crib and using all her effort, picked me up. That was all she was able to do.

But just then the kitchen door opened, and the Lord entered with a few of His Disciples. She handed me to the Lord Jesus, and He picked me up and raised me over His head and held me in such a way that I became filled with joy and peace, and I was kicking my legs and having a wonderful time. That was the end of the dream.

I knew that the Lord cared for me. Those around me were unable to, even though they might want to. It reminded me of the Lord saying, "When I call you, I call you by name, you are carved on the palm of my hand, and even though a mother may forget her child, I will never forget you."

So that was my dream, and the Lord came forth, and I knew in the midst of the feelings of abandonment and solitude, the Lord cared for me.

Another healing vision I had involved my caring for the Lord and my acceptance of my role in His agony. I was driving from Ontario, Canada en route home to Fitchburg, Massachusetts and I was saying the Rosary. I pray to Our Blessed Mother to be intercessor so that the people who come to healing services will be touched by the Lord's compassionate healing power. I never turn on the radio in the car, but I pray the Rosary, and I also pray it for all those who have specifically asked me for prayers. It was Christmas Day, so I sang "Happy birthday, Jesus." People must have though I was nuts!

It then struck me that I wanted, like all the saints, to experience the ugliness of sin so that, while thinking the happy thought of Jesus' birth, I would gain an insight into His passion and death. There was a cassette player in the car, and I inserted a tape that lay nearby and out came the words, "My passion is your triumph."

At that moment I had the vision of being close to the Lord in the Garden of Gethsemane. I stood next to Jesus to see what part I have in this. There was the Lord in agony, and I cried because I saw images which showed that I was a part of that. I was responsible for my sinfulness. From that came a cleansing and the coming again of the Lord into my life.

Does the Lord speak to you today? Of course. Do we listen for the voice of the Lord? Maybe. But I guarantee you, from my own experience, if you ask to hear the voice of the Lord, then you will hear it speaking to you at a time and in places that you least expect — maybe in the depth of your heart, maybe in the silence of your sorrow, maybe in the joy of a rejoicing. He may speak to you through people who offend you; you may hear His voice in the criminal that everyone condemns, or in the voice of children who are part of God's wisdom. No matter where we look — as long as we do look and seek — we will find.

What He Did Then, He Does Now

The Lord does today what He did when He was walking those dusty streets of all the countries He traveled, and I will share an experience which occurred within my family to dramatize the parallel. Recall in Matthew 8:14-15 that Peter's mother-in-law was sick in bed with a fever when Jesus came to the house. What did He do when He learned that? He touched her hand, and helped her up, and the fever left her. Can that happen today? Yes.

I have a nephew who has five children. I visit often. One day I saw that my four and one half year old grandniece was sick, her beautiful hair all knotted and sweaty. She was asleep on the rug with her coat on, and I was told she had a fever. Her mother, a nurse, had scheduled to take her to the doctor that evening. When she woke up and saw me she was surprised and happy, as we are very loving of one another. She then curled up at my feet and went to sleep. When she woke up later I said to her, "You are not feeling well, how about if we ask Jesus to take that fever away so you can go out and play?" "Oh, yes," she said.

So I blessed her with blessed oil, and I said a brief prayer of command: "Fever, I command you in the name of Jesus Christ leave her right now." As I was praying, her features changed, light came back into her eyes, the fever left, and she went out to play.

The Lord preaches today; He teaches today; He heals today. And it is not complicated. We do not have to say elaborate prayers with well-balanced phrases. We do not have to go on and on in prayer. We do not have to shout and wave our hands around. God does not need a hearing aid. Did He make a lot of noise when He healed Peter's mother? No, He took her by the hand in silence. He is the Word, and people can just come and touch the hem of His cloak, and they are healed because He is the Word and the Light and the Way.

One way of healing is through a prayer of command. Jesus, filled with pity and compassion, reached out and touched the leper and commanded he be made clean. It was a healing from authority, with the assumption that it would happen because He was saying it and He was the Word of God. If we make command prayers in the name of Jesus Christ, He will do today what He did then.

For Parents, A Special Power and Duty

Parents have a special power through Christ for praying over their children, and a special obligation to do so. Children are especially open to be healed. They are especially vulnerable to both good and evil. The Lord told us this, and so, if they are sick, you as parents are the ones most called to pray over them, because you love them the most. Love has a great part in healing, so reach out to your sick children and pray the sickness out. Take authority over that illness in the name of Jesus Christ. Pray over your children, asking Jesus to be the one to touch them, heal them and love them.

Never be discouraged if your prayer seems not to be answered in the way you expect. God always hears our sincere and loving prayers, and He always answers them in ways beyond our expectation. Pray always with perseverance, joy and expectation that healing might be channeled through you unto all seeking God's help and health.

Christ, The Divine Physician

Jesus healed in different ways. He accepted and He utilized all the medical knowledge of His time. He used saliva because it was then determined it had medicinal benefits. He used oil. He used water to cleanse. He used diverse ways to show us that in healing there is no formula. Some of you might say, "Teach me some techniques." There are no techniques. What does the Lord say to do? He says, "Do what I did, pray, and pray in My name." That is what He taught His Apostles. That is what He is teaching us.

Chapter 3

FORGIVENESS: THE SPIRIT OF JESUS, THE ESSENCE OF HEALING

Praise You Father. We ask that You send Your Spirit to dwell in us, so that in all we do and say, Your love will shine forth. We ask also that You fill us with wisdom to lead Your flock into a closer relationship with You. We ask that You forgive us our faults and failures and let us see our weaknesses in the reflection of Your love for us. Show us how to forgive ourselves so that we may be able to forgive those who have hurt us. Keep us safe from the traps of the evil one, especially the traps of seeking power and material possessions. Let us use the gifts You have given us fully, but always in the knowledge that the power comes from You, through Your Spirit, the Advocate, whom Your son, Our Lord, Jesus Christ promised us. We ask, through Your Son, Our Lord, Jesus Christ, that Your will be done as You would have it done. We make this prayer through Christ Our Lord. AMEN

A Scriptural Teaching

This chapter is a teaching on forgiveness, and I would like to begin with the text on "Brotherly Correction" from Matthew 18:

If your brother does something wrong, go and have it out with him alone, between your two selves. (Now, since the self is the deepest part of our personality, the instruction here is to do it intimately.)

If he listens to you, you have won back your brother. If he does not listen, take one or two others along with you. But if he refuses to listen to these, report to the community; and if he refuses to listen to the community, treat him like a pagan or a tax collector. I tell you solemnly whatever you bind on earth shall be considered bound in heaven; and whatever you loose on earth, shall be considered loosed in heaven. For where two or three meet in my name, I shall be there with them.

Then Peter went up to him and said, "Lord, how often must I forgive my brother if he wrongs me? As often as seven times?" Jesus answered, "Not seven, I tell you, but seventy-seven times."

That is the fullness of divine measure.

And let us also reflect upon Ephesians 4: "Be friends with one another and kind, forgiving each other as readily as God forgave you in Christ."

Forgive as He Did

In the previous chapter, we considered the miracles of Christ's healing ministry on earth as models of what we, as followers of His, can be called and empowered through Him to accomplish. But we must also look to His ministry for the key which unlocks the door to healing, without which we cannot be healed, and without which we cannot become healers.

Now if I were to ask you, what word did the Lord use most often in the three years that he taught and preached and healed, what would you say? You might respond with the word "love," since God is Love. And you might say "light," since Jesus is the Light of the World. And you might say the "way," for the same reason.

However, the words most often used in the ministry of Jesus on earth are "mercy" and "forgiveness." So there must be something important about these terms. Forgiveness is an aspect of love. Jesus forgave, and we must do the same. Without forgiveness and without the compassionate love of Jesus, there is no healing. Forgiveness is the one condition essential to the healing of ourselves and to the functioning of ourselves as channels of Jesus' healing and love.

By being unforgiving, we remain in the bondage from which Christ seeks to free us. By being unforgiving, we set ourselves up to fail by not allowing the spirit of Christ to shine within us and shine forth from us unto others.

If we believe that Jesus has invited us to follow Him, if we wish to carry the banner of Jesus, the victorious One, to others then we are to do what He did in His day. He forgave.

Unforgiveness is the most daunting obstacle to healing. I will give you an example. One day I said a healing of ancestry Mass in a private home, and afterwards I asked if there was anyone in pain. One man said, "Yes," lower back pain, twenty-four hours a day for a number of years." I asked if he wanted to be prayed over, and he said yes. So I put my hand on his back, and everyone joined in, and we prayed over him. After a while, I said, "How do you feel now?" He said, "No better, no change."

Now, I was surprised because usually when I pray over someone to be relieved of pain, it happens — with migraine headaches, arthritis, whatever it is, and that is why I am grateful to the Lord for this gift. I was stumped. So I said, "Do you want me to pray a little more?" "Well, if you want, go ahead," he replied. So we prayed some more. I knew nothing was happening, so I stopped again and asked if there was any change.

"There is no change," he said, and he was kind of angry at this point. "No change, same as when you started." What occurred to me then was that he had a block here. He should be healed. I asked: "Is there anyone who hurt you that you have not forgiven?" And with an angry expression he said, "Yes, there is."

"Well, I replied, "We can pray all the time, but the Lord cannot answer that prayer unless you are a forgiving person. Now if you want we can pray with you for the gift of forgiveness from the Holy Spirit." I explained to him that forgiveness is a gift, it is "for giving." With the help of the Holy Spirit we can give up the bitterness, the anger, sometimes the hatred, the resentment we hold. I added that we would pray for the gift if he so wished, and that if he did, then he would bc healed. His answer was "No."

I had to respect his negative answer. That was his choice. He was left with his pain. It seems like a terrible choice, but he was just not ready for the gift the Lord wanted to give him. He was not healed.

I have seen it over and over again. If you do not forgive, you remain unhealed and in pain. You forgive, you are healed.

How important is forgiveness? Consider that the one prayer the Lord gave us through the Apostles — The Lord's Prayer — contains instruction on this topic. Right in the middle of that prayer there is the adverb "as." We petition for His forgiveness "as" — in the same measure that we forgive others. Without that, the rest, thy kingdom come, does not happen. And our daily bread somehow falls short if we are unforgiving people.

Are There Help and Hope for the Unforgiving?

Many times we simply say we cannot forgive, and that, of course, may be true. And if we find ourselves in that state, all we need do is ask for the gift of forgiveness from the Holy Spirit. We can pray for that gift.

Another and related way to forgive when our hearts are closed to forgiveness is to ask the Lord to show us what it is that He loves about the person we cannot forgive. Remember, again, God created every one of us in His likeness and in His image.

I will share with you how I learned to forgive.

Once when I was in the Philippines, I was making my way to a barrio chapel to celebrate Mass when it dawned on me that I was preaching forgiveness while being unforgiving toward persons who really hurt me. I asked the Lord for help.

Then I recalled He gave us the new law, — "love one another as I have loved you." "Well," I said, "Lord, that is nice, but I just cannot love that person, and I do not know how You can either. So I am asking You to share with me the way in which You love that person so I can love him in the same way."

Then, in my mind's eye, I saw the person who hurt me the most. It was like a coat of candle wax which covered him had all melted away. I felt the warmth of the Lord's compassionate love come through me. I could see then that our Father had placed in this person's heart, too, the Spirit of Christ. What could I do? I could not go against the Lord because I had just asked Him to help me.

So that is another way in which forgiveness comes about — when we lift up an unselfish prayer. When we are humble enough to say to the Lord that we need some assistance in doing this. Then we remain open to the word of God coming through the Holy Spirit, Who is the Giver of Life. Then we are revived, and we see clearly that we are all broken people, and unless we forgive those who have hurt us, we will not be forgiven.

There are two ways we can develop in life. We can either become bitter or better. There is a choice, we have that choice. We can become bitter, or we can become better. When we get into a prayer stance with sincerity, generosity, humility and honesty, we are open to be healed. And that certainly is choosing the better. This approach always works for the hurts that are foremost in our consciousness.

Dealing with Suppressed Memories

Sometimes, however, the hurt and the people who hurt us are buried in our memory deep within the unconscious, and the only way to get in touch with them is through prayer. When we decide we want to forgive everyone in our lives, we can only forgive those persons whom we are conscious of having been injured by in our past. The Holy Spirit, if we pray, will help us forgive the others.

We just need to ask the Lord for help, and He will speak to us. When He does, and when He knows we are ready to forgive, He will send us the memory of those "terrible" persons in our past. And we will hold those names in front of us; they will surface, like a little film, showing all the ways we believe we have been hurt by these individuals. When it unwinds to its finish, we will be able to say, "I forgive you, one hundred percent in the name of Jesus Christ."

I offer you a case in point.

At a conference on healing ministry I attended at Staten Island, many people were prayed over by prayer teams. One such team consisted of Father Francis MacNutt, Barbara Shlemon, Fr. Paul Schaaf, Sister Jeanne Hill and myself. Every person we prayed over was overpowered by the Spirit and rested in the Spirit. The Lord decides who is overpowered by the Spirit, as it is His way of dealing with people directly.

One nun who was prayed over — a missionary from Africa — rested in the spirit for about two and one half hours. The next day, when Fr. MacNutt began his talk, she said, "Wait a minute, I must tell you all what happened to me when I rested in the Spirit for over two hours." And she related the following:

"When I went to Africa to join the Sisters as a missionary, I was the youngest one, and I was the last one to be there. The other Sisters had been there for many years. I figured the first thing I was going to do was to learn the language so I could communicate with these people. So I did that, and after I did, every time someone came to the convent, they would ask specifically for me.

But many of the sisters became jealous because I was being called so frequently to serve these people. When I was resting in the Spirit, every person who had hurt me in my past surfaced in my memory, and I let the memory float there, and the way the person hurt me came back to me as if on a film.

At the end I said, 'Lord, I forgive this person one hundred percent in your name.' Then another person would surface and so on. Some of these people who had been hurtful I had forgotten completely about. Well, when I finished it dawned on me, 'This is nice, I forgave everybody, but what about me?' At that moment I felt the deepest kind of peace I have ever experienced."

I believe the peace came to that nun because she was forgiven one hundred percent in the same measure she had forgiven those who had injured her. This is a powerful example of how the Lord works. He dealt with this woman directly, so she might be freed to be healed

We All Are Hurting People

Since we are all born in human brokenness, since we are not perfect, we are all going to experience hurt, and we are going to hurt others. If we had the strength of the Lord, we would respond to injurious words and deeds by reaching out and touching the person or persons in positive, gentle and loving ways. We generally do not have that strength, but we can ask the Lord for it, and He will give it to us.

Many years ago my mother told me "Little babies do not cry for nothing. Something is wrong, and you have to find out what that is."

In my years of professional counseling I have found that we adults are like little babies. If we are hurting, we are going to strike out. When we say he hurt me or she hurt me, that is really not true. What is true, perhaps, is that they provided an occasion for us to respond with hurt feelings. We create our own feelings. No one hurts us. We forge our own emotions of hurt.

Sometimes we keep hurting people because we cannot stand keeping all that hurt within ourselves. We fail to see we own those injuries; we blame others; finally when there is no one else to blame, we blame God.

When we have finished blaming God, we have only ourselves. At that point maybe we can look at the hurts we have created within ourselves and realize that they are really not of God.

The Lord intends us to be in touch with our own goodness. If all we see within ourselves are injuries and limitations, we tend to defend them and pass on to others our hurts. Access the spirit of Christ within yourself; search it out; learn the truth of who you are, and you will have a new strength that says its okay for other people to be the way they are, it is okay for them to lash out at us because they are hurting. I will not retaliate, but I will ask myself the pastoral question, "How best can I help this person who is in pain? Perform the loving gesture, give the loving word, be the loving presence, and those kind of responses spell pastoral, they spell healing.

Today is the time for peace, and peace comes when we are honest with ourselves, with others and with God. If we have the loving attitude, there is no way we can interpret anything others are saying to us or doing to us as hurting us. We can only see it as a person in pain passing on his pain to us.

We can set ourselves up to become physically ill if we are unforgiving persons. We often react to perception of hurt with anger, frustration, hatred, fear, guilt, plans for retaliation and revenge. The result is emotional confusion, spiritual deterioration and depression. Our so-perceived wounds fester within us, slowly destroying us. Where there should be light, where there should be the Kingdom of God abiding within us, there is, instead, darkness. These negative and destructive feelings, these resentments erode our spiritual, mental and physical health. These "hurts," if unforgiven have an insidious and far-reaching impact on our very lives.

Pursue peace through loving. Jesus has promised us His peace which can be found in the center of the whirlpool of our activities where there is no movement, but only calm. There may be turbulence; there may be people shouting at us, there may be events going wrong, but we are centered where there is no tumult. We stand firmly in the peace of Jesus.

The Pain of Rejection

Rejection is one of the major hurts, whether real or imagined. It has been demonstrated that even the unborn can feel rejection in the mother's womb. If that child enters life and remains unhealed of that feeling, the burden will last a lifetime. Sometimes when we are praying over a person, we can visualize the moment the unborn was hurt by rejection.

I once had a baptism of an adopted baby. There is part of the liturgy of the Sacrament of Baptism which is exorcism. It occurred to me that this child was going to cry out when I said those prayers, so I shared that with the family. I said, "Do not be afraid, but he is going to scream as if I were strangling him, because we are entering into a conflict between good and evil, between God, Jesus Christ Our Savior, and Satan, who wants this child."

I incorporated into this prayer, what I saw to be the situation — that this adopted child had been rejected. He was born of an unmarried woman, and the father did not want the baby. The mother lived with her parents, and they told her she should not keep the infant. He just did not have a chance, with all these people around him who had rejected him.

And what I did, I served as a proxy. I took the child's place, and I forgave all the people who rejected him, so that he would be free. This act of forgiveness was a way within the Sacrament of Baptism, to give the baby freedom to be healed. Today he is such a well-adjusted young man. Even before a child has the use of reason, he or she has many feelings. Adopted children are especially vulnerable to the pain of rejection.

Following is an anecdote offered by Patricia A. Kelly in illustration of Fr. Al's observations on healing the feelings of rejection of adopted children:

"We adopted our son from a Third World country when he was four and a half, after he had been living in an orphanage for nearly a year. He frequently experienced night terrors, and for several months after he came home to us, while sleeping fitfully he would call out in his native language the words for 'mother' and 'father.' After a while, he would use the English equivalents, and his bad dreams continued. Sometimes he would walk in his sleep, always coming directly to one of us or both of us whatever room we happened to be in at the time, as if to be sure that we were still there.

When Father Al came to our home to say a Mass of intergenerational healing, we could not construct any family tree for the birth ancestors of our son. We only knew that whatever the realities of a past unknown to us, he was experiencing pain, anger and grief and fear of abandonment.

While sitting next to Father Al at the dining room table during that Mass, our son was the most peaceful we had ever seen him — quiet and restful. Immediately after the Mass, those terrible nightmares stopped, and the frequency of sleepwalking diminished dramatically. Today, two years later, the disturbances have disappeared.

A few weeks later we brought our son to a healing Mass at the La Salette Shrine in Attleboro, where he was anointed by Father Andre Patenaude, a La Salette missionary. As we were being prayed over by Father Pat, I had a sense that our son needed to be reconnected in a positive way to his conception and birth. I then left the chapel, went to the La Salette book store and purchased a copy of a book for children entitled, Before You Were Born *by Joan Lowery Nixon.*

The message of this beautiful little story is that a child is dreamed of by God, wanted and loved by God even before his conception. The book details the development of the child in the womb through birth, with every step being infused with the sentiment that he is a wanted child., that he is a precious child. I read this book with our son; he cried, and I think those were healing tears. I have shared with other adoptive parents this experience of recreating the gestation and birth of our son through the perspective of a loving God. They have agreed that such an exercise has had more benefit than anything they have tried to do or say about what the child perceives as rejection by his birth family.

The Unborn, The Stillborn Need to Forgive

It is not only the adopted child who needs to forgive. The unbaptized aborted child, the unbaptized stillborn child, the miscarried infant have the same requirement. Remember, they are all created in God's image and likeness. Those who were never baptized, never named, never given an opportunity to live with their brothers and sisters — they are all hurt people, hurt and rejected, and someone needs to ask them for forgiveness. This can be done in proxy.

For example, at an intergenerational healing Mass I lift up within a family all the children never baptized, and as a community of faith we can lift them up to the Lord through a baptism of desire, and we should assign names to these little children who were never on earth. Then they belong to the family of God, and they have the right to heaven to be with the angels and saints, and so we ask in our prayer to have the angels guide them into Paradise. We find when this is done, peace is restored to a family.

Dr. Kenneth McAll, who has written extensively on illness and the healing power of the Eucharist, introduced me to the importance of this concept. In his book entitled *Healing the Family Tree*, he says: "Just as we lovingly name our own children at baptism, we should also name a 'lost' child to express how it belongs to us and is loved. Sometimes a mother or a brother or sister will know the intended name of such a baby; at other times the Lord gives us a name as we pray."

Dr. McAll relates that during a Mass he attended which was intended for the raising up of an aborted child in the baptism of desire, there was a squeak of the church door during communion. When he turned around (Dr. McAll has visions) he saw a young woman, about age 22, walk down the aisle and up to the cross on the altar. He saw the Lord step down and embrace her as she wept. At the end of the consecration prayers, the scene disappeared.

The woman who prayed for her aborted child confirmed that the child would be age 22 that year if she had lived. She also confirmed Dr. McAll's description of the young woman as conforming with the physical features of her family.

Based on his visions, Dr. McAll concluded the following:

"Some people believe that all babies go straight to God when they die. This is indeed so if they have been loved and prayed for on earth. I have witnessed over six hundred cases of babies who had died continuing to grow up at the same rate as they would have grown in life. Each baby has its own guardian angel waiting for a time of love and committal to God; the angel then has permission to act. And I disagree with those who argue that if a pregnancy has lasted only a few weeks the baby was not formed and does not count. My experience of 'seeing' these babies in their own age group proves to me the truth of God's word 'Before I formed you in the womb I knew you' (Jer 1.5 and Psalm 139.13). Such babies were real people with souls and memories of the loving God who had once handled them."[2]

The Stories of 'Bertha' and 'Mary' and 'Mary Elizabeth'

What all this is telling us is that no matter what those pro-abortion people and those who perform abortions do, they cannot foil God's plans. The child is intended by God to live a certain age, and the child continues to grow. They think they have killed the child, but you cannot kill the soul. The Lord's own children are not to be tortured in those ways, and so He intervenes, and they continue to grow. Isn't that amazing?

I was giving a conference at the St. Boniface Medical Center in St. Boniface, Canada, when a certain employee stopped to ask if I would pray for her husband. She said that he would go into periodic rages. So I went to their house for dinner and prayed over him, and then I asked if she wished me to pray over her also. She said yes, and in the middle of my prayer I was moved to say, "Now I lift you up in the baptism of desire, and I give you the name Bertha."

Then, when I had finished praying, this woman said, "How did you know?" I said, "Know what?" She replied, "That I had a miscarriage, and it was a girl." I did not know that, but the Holy Spirit takes over and inspires. This mother did not feel blame or shame, but she rejoiced that someone came into her life and asked Jesus to bring His perfect humanity to bear and to heal a situation.

Following is the story of 'Mary,' as offered by Patricia A. Kelly.

One day, after I had read Father Robert DeGrandis' book entitled Intergenerational Healing *and had been reflecting on what he, too, says about the need to have all infants baptized, unborn and born, I closed my eyes to rest. As I did, I saw this young woman, her back to me, walking down the aisle of the church where I at-*

*tended Mass, passing by the pew where I generally sit, and where
our prayer group convenes. Her slim, long-legged build, her long
fair hair, reminded me of my father's side of our family. She was
dressed in the fashion that is contemporary for her age group, wear-
ing a white cotton tunic topic and a yellow and brown paisley print
jumper.*

*As she neared the altar, she turned left, toward the statue of
Our Blessed Mother holding the Christ Child. She paused, putting
her hand on the corner of the railing, as if she were waiting for
something to happen. As she did, I was prompted to name her
"Mary," and lift her up in a baptism of desire. She then steadily
approached the statue with a confident step, and the "dream"?
ended.*

*Now I do not know specifically and intellectually if there were
any miscarriages, still births or abortions in our family fifteen or
twenty years ago. But my heart told me that this young woman
belonged in our family and that our Lord and Our Blessed Mother
wanted her named and baptized."*

*Following is the story of "Mary Elizabeth," as offered by her
mother, Marian J. Desrosiers of Buzzards Bay, Massachusetts,
who is an assistant diocesan director of a Pro Life Apostolate:*

*"Joe and I were expecting our third child about 12 years ago.
I had a very difficult pregnancy and when our son, Marc Edward,
was born, he had a serious birth defect known as diaphramatic
hernia. He underwent major surgery and died a day later.*

*Joe and I began to look closer at our lives and realized what
was most important to us were our children. They were a gift from
God for only a brief time, and we were to enjoy them and count
each day with them a blessing.*

*Time moved on, and I delivered our son, Lee, our fourth child.
He was healthy.*

During my fifth pregnancy, my doctors assured me everything was fine, but I sensed that something was wrong. And at the beginning of the ninth month, our daughter, Mary Elizabeth, died in my womb.

Joe and I were both determined she would be handled with dignity during all the medical procedures which were to follow. We decided to wait for my own labor to begin, which took an additional three-week period. We prayed with our family.

Mary was born breech, feet first. The sight of her little feet left an imprint upon my memory. Joe insisted that he and I spend some time with our daughter. In a private room we held her and loved her and we lifted her up in the baptism of desire, naming her. After that, we were able to let go of her and place her in the hands of the Lord.

The following day, doctors and nurses came to express sympathy and to say how pleased and surprised they were by the dignity and love we showed our daughter. They said they had seen a recent increase in parents rejecting their infants born with birth defects.

I began to realize that perfection for children was the message society was sending out — if not perfect, then not wanted. And I realized, too that we needed to speak out and reclaim the dignity all children and all individuals deserve to be given no matter what their condition in life.

In memory of Mary Elizabeth, I had donations sent to Birthright, and as a token of their appreciation, I received a pair of tiny golden baby's feet, the symbol of pro life. I knew in my heart it was Mary's way of saying, "Speak for them, Mom, for they cannot speak for themselves." I began to receive telephone calls from women who lost children, women who were in difficult pregnancies, women who had abortions. I shared my experiences with them and felt unconditional love for them. In order for the healing process to begin, I encouraged them to name their babies, pray for their babies at Mass, and these actions led many back to the Sacrament of Reconciliation. You see, no matter how a mother loses her child, she always blames herself. She needs God's love and mercy to touch her, to show her how to forgive herself and be free from guilt.

I would like to tell you one of the calls I received. I was in my fifth month of pregnancy with my sixth child, Stephen Andrew, who is now two years old, and a weeping mother called. She, too, was in her fifth month, but doctors told her she was carrying a severely deformed fetus.

She was swollen with an additional 25 pounds of fluid, and she could not even lie down at night. She was told that the fetus could not survive long outside the womb, that it had no sexual identity. Her life was not in danger, but doctors strongly suggested that the pregnancy be terminated. She asked me for guidance.

I prayed to the Holy Spirit for the right words and I was prompted to share with her my experiences. When I finished she indicated she was amazed to hear that this was a child within her. She asked, "I will have this child for all eternity?" I said, "Yes, a beautiful baby boy or girl will wait for you in heaven to share eternity with you." She cried because no one had even called her fetus a child.

I encouraged her to speak with her clergy, her family and doctors. I promised Joe and I would pray often for her and her family. I told her I would always be there to talk with her, and I said goodbye.

Two months after Stephen was born, I received a congratulatory call from this woman. She told me she continued with her pregnancy and after much suffering and great personal sacrifice, she delivered a baby boy early in her seventh month, and he lived only one hour. She and her husband shared that hour with their son. She said she was glad they were able to love him and treat him with dignity. She said her son taught them so much about life, and she was proud he died in his parents' arms. She said she felt such peace, despite the high price paid. She said she became angry when hospital personnel referred to her son as a fetus, and she told them to stop doing that, that he was a beautiful little boy.

I would like to share with you what we might call the final chapter of the story of that telephone call. A year ago on Mother's Day I was at Mass when I saw a young mother with a baby in her arms and two other children next to her. The children's grandmother appeared not to be feeling well, so I offered to watch her children, and she handed me the baby. I held this beautiful two-month old boy in my arms and saw that his brother and sister regarded him with great joy. When the mother returned at the end of Mass she asked, "Are you Marian?" I said, "Yes," and apologized because I did not recognize her. She told me she was the woman I had spoken with whose little boy lived only one hour. The baby I was holding was her newborn son. Because she had done the right thing, she and her husband had courage to try again. God responded with the beautiful gift of this perfect baby. What a joy it was for me to meet this family and for God to allow me to hold their son. I looked at this baby's smile through my own tears and the Lord's words rang in my ears: "Amen, I say to you, whatever you did for one of these least brothers of mine, you did for me."

This is why I do pro life work — to restore the dignity to our children and our families. If we do not, the very fabric of family life will be torn away. We have only to look at the facts. Since Roe v. Wade, child abuse, which was supposed to decrease with the decrease in birth of unwanted children, has increased alarmingly. The most dangerous place to live now is in the mother's womb. During a twenty-year period the children killed by abortion far outnumbers those killed in all the wars in which this nation has fought.

Our Lord will judge us as a nation on this issue. It is our problem because we are all part of His family, and it is our brothers and sisters who are being killed by abortion. These values, thank the Lord, are not shared by all nations.

I have a deep devotion to Our Lady of Guadalupe, the Protectress of Life, who, when she left her miraculous image on the cloak of Juan Diego in 1531, was carrying within her the Christ child. I have visited her shrine in Mexico City on her feast day, December

12, and have been awed by the devotion of families to her. These poor people of our world display a deep reverence for Our Lord and Blessed Mother. They sleep in the shrine and in streets outside to get a chance to pay homage. It is not poverty and over-populations that have hurt family life and values, but greed and selfishness."

Healing the Hurts of Abortion

There is a special healing needed for a person who has had an abortion. I can tell you from my experience that every one whom I have met who has had an abortion and has not been healed — displays signs of something deep within that is amiss. The spirit, the emotions are distressed.

The late Father John Lazanski, a Franciscan priest who was assigned to the Arch Street Mission in Boston, always offered to pray over someone who had had an abortion. One day he was telling me exactly how he proceeded in prayer.

I was impressed with his prayer, and I told him that more than two thousand professionals who are members of the Association of Christian Therapists deal every day with this issue. So when the association met in Scottsdale, Arizona, I persuaded him to present a talk which included his prayer. It is excerpted as follows:

Rev. John Lazanski, O. F. M.: On Inner Healing

"The ministry at the shrine is very, very intense. We estimate that between 35,0000 to 40,000 pass through the doors each week, and we have thirty-five Masses on weekends. In 1970 I went back to school to pick up a degree in pastoral psychology, because I realized my ministry was not that effective… Working with people — I still found — I was using psychological tools with the traditional classical priestly background — I still found I was ineffective. I guess I then gradually became a charismatic or something. I attended the workshop in Staten Island with an open mind, with a little skepticism, perhaps. And there I was introduced to Father Francis MacNutt… and the Linn Brothers, Barbara Shlemon, and one of my favorites, Agnes Sanford — I read every book of hers I could get my hands on. I guess I have read hundreds of books on healing.

So at the shrine, I began to pray, as well as counsel. And I would find people coming back in a week or two and saying, 'Thank-you, Father.' I wondered, why the thanks? People were starting to phone in every day for an appointment for an inner healing. And I said, 'What is going on.?' People in prayer groups started to make a noise: 'There is an inner healer down in Arch Street.' Inner healing for me was a new direction, a new route, a new road. So I asked the Spirit to guide me.

And some of the stuff that came was just unbelievable. One woman, her husband blew out his brains — a police officer — and for years she had been going to psychiatric treatment, and there was no release. She would come in, and I had to take her into that room where he blew out his brains, and she was released. She was just born anew, filled with joy and peace.

Another woman lived with an alcoholic butcher. And he practiced his cutting art by trying to butcher her —for years, she stayed because there were four children. She was a zombie emotionally. She would go to Mass, and it was just a dead thing. She was dead. Today she is one of the coordinators of my public healing ministry. And she is just bubbling and joyful, just full of life and love.

And there was a woman conceived out of wedlock who was told a story by her mother. The mother made pretense she was married and hubby died. And she discovered this when she was sixteen — so this emotional self-image was, "I am bad," and there is need for deliverance for this, and she was healed. And there are kids sexually abused by their parents, siblings, and you know the chaotic state of people, and they are coming back, and I am finding out they are thanking me. Crazy?

So I realized, Lord You are doing something here, so just keep on doing it, whatever it is.

There was one woman, born in Italy. The father was on the war front, and there were many kids, and she eventually became a prostitute. She met a G. I. and came over here. And in Italy she had an abortion. She came to this country and could not have children. And then the sister's husband conceived a child out of wedlock, and this woman made believe this baby was her child... the craziness of our modern, broken, sick, devil-ridden world!

And more and more abortion cases were coming in. One woman had had three abortions through three marriages. One husband was a sadist, another a playboy, another a psychopath. Drug addicts would come in. So I told myself, you have to be creative in your prayer. I remember reading Father MacNutt's book, and he said you take counseling for fifteen minutes and then you pray. And try to get down to roots and patterns. And I found that the people coming in to me did not have one or two or three traumas like Ruth Stapleton says, but I have been finding eight scars, eighteen scars, twenty-seven, forty-seven scars.

So I told myself, a doctor who has a patient coming in, who has been slashed seventeen times, does he suture only three gashes or five? So I said, analogously, he takes care of every wound and hurt. If you are doing inner healing, all these scars are in the psyche... , on the unconscious and conscious levels, in every cell of the body, in every organ. How do you deal with all of this? Realizing man is tripartite and tri-dimensional, I said the Lord has come to heal us totally, so you might lead life to the full, so he is healing us, not only spiritually in the confessional, but physically and emotionally.

So I would invite the Lord Jesus to be living and present, plug into Him in the Spirit and ask the Spirit to anoint me... And with abortions, there is an incompleteness, and I always go through a deliverance with abortions.

In addition to this, since I am a priest, after doing all the cleansing and the negativities, I replace them with positive things, and I end up finally with the power of the Sacrament of Reconciliation. Then I finally bring in the Holy Spirit to do the releasing. So I do a real holistic job. So it takes me usually from one session to six or seven.

My prayers are unpredictable. I try to pick up the roots and see how many prayers they need. Normally I take them through the stairway of life, from Ruth Stapleton — from zero, conception, up to age five. I have the transference from the parents through the third, fourth generations, physical, spiritual, psychological — I slash these — so they will go to the Spirit, so no longer are there transmissions for future generation. And there on in, thanks to the insights with our paraconferences — Barbara Shlemon is just beautiful — her insights, and of course, Father MacNutt, and all the others who are in there sharing — I incorporate this, and it just comes out from the well within me. All this stuff going in, and it comes out, and it just pops into my head, and I pray.

Having a Freudian type of background, I believe the first three years are the critical ones, when… the personality, orientations are pretty well solidified. The psychiatrists tell us that by the time you are six years old, you have had a billion experiences. So your core and peripheral personality have become rigid. You are going to be a winner or a loser in life. Then I go up to the year five, and then up to the present moment. I take the significant relationship with the father and mother, and from there on in the siblings, sometimes the boys — the brother, at puberty might have broken into the girl's bedroom, stripped and manipulated her or even had coitus with her. These are the scars of family life you come up with in inner healing.

They are the realities you do not sweep under the rock. They are there, and you deal with them. And you heal them, you heal people, that is what we are there for.

Then I take all the significant relationships, the traumas. Some have been through three marriages, some women are prostitutes, so I say a prayer for that. Some individuals are diffuse in their sexual identity — they are bisexual, and I will work on this. So whatever comes up, I try to cope with it. I would say my success is roughly eighty-five to ninety percent with the cases I deal with. It is the most demanding kind of ministry...

I can have a deliverance, and then the Sacrament of Reconciliation. I will use deliverance in abortion, specifically naming the spirit of abortion. If I am uncertain about a modality for healing, I will use multiple ones to make sure there is a healing taking place. That is why at the end I will also use the Sacrament of Reconciliation — always as a priest, if you come in for inner healing, this is the final big healing."

Rev. John Lazanski: On Healing for Abortion

"In my ministry, I have had many coming in for healing of memories — as it is called. And among these I have had women who have had abortions. I will share my techniques with my confreres in the Association of Christian Therapists who made a request. I have made a tape for them to use to help heal people because of the endemic proportions within our nation of abortion. Now I will describe my prayer technique:

I have before me a client, let us give her the name Jeannette. She is in her thirties. She confided to me that her husband died about a year ago, and in the interim she had a relationship with someone, and during that she became pregnant. Eventually she made a decision to have an abortion. So with the client I usually I try to tell them:

Jeannette, we are going to try now to go back in memory and picture the place where you had your abortion — clinic, hospital, whatever, make it as graphic and specific as possible.

There you are, and this time, Jeannette, I want you to bring Jesus into the situation, and His mother Mary. And picture Jesus with His handsome dark face, and with His dignity, but He is so approachable, you know. He is our brother, our elder brother.

He has come into our midst to deal with our hurts and our wounds. For He said, "I have come so you could have life and have it to the full." Extortionists, even murderers, even women who were adulterers came to Him, and somehow they could always feel at ease with Jesus. So there is no need for you to panic. Jesus is here to heal and help, not condemn.

Mary, Our Mother, before Jesus died and He was up on that cross, He looked down at John who symbolizes all of us and said, "Son, behold your mother." So Mary is God's last gift to us. And Jeannette, Mary is your mother, and she is right here now with her white frock, her blue mantle and Her beautiful face. She loves you with a Mother's love, full of understanding, compassion.

At this moment, we want to picture Jesus as Lord and Savior, but also as Divine Physician. And right now the process of the abortion has been completed, and they are taking out the embryo. And Jesus intervenes and says, "Pardon me, sir, but I will take this child if you don't mind."

Praise You Lord.

And since Mary is also the mother of this child, Jesus tenderly, lovingly hands this child over to Mary. And Mary, being the loving mother that she is, takes this child, takes a clean white swab, begins to wipe its forehead, its eyes, its nose, its cheeks, lips, neck, turns it over lovingly and gently and wipes back of the head, ears, the neck, shoulder plates, back, buttocks, legs, turns it over, gets a clean cloth and washes the arms, armpits, the hands, little fingers, then the chest, tummy, pubic area, upper leg areas, knees, lower legs, and then the little feet. Then she puts a clean cloth over its midriff. Being the Mother she is, she takes this child, with all the love and tenderness she has as a beautiful mother — to her heart.

And the child can feel all the vibrations of that maternal love, feels all the love, security, acceptance she has a right to. You see, human life is a miracle, a gift from God. Mary knows this. God makes us. The parents, sometimes, interactions, might commit sin. They might call it a mistake, an accident. But we are never, never an accident. We receive our being, existence, from the Creative Power, the living God. And God says, "I have known you all eternity and loved you with an everlasting love, and I have given you a name." And Mary knows this. She is a woman full of wisdom, the Word of God, the Knowledge of God. She knows about us in our radical worthwhileness, our personhood, our dignity.

She praises God for this creation. She thanks Him. And now that the child has received this type of warmth and acceptance, we know that Jesus died for it. He has redeemed all humanity by His dying and His rising.

There is need to take away the scars and the fears that a child who had died unbaptized might go to limbo or God knows where. So right now, I go through a spiritual baptism, and I baptize the child, which in a sense gives it a right now to go to heaven. And after this, with Jesus there and with Mary, we have an open scenario with a mother.

And I tell the mother, Let us give the name "Mary" to this child. And, mother, I want you to address this child in the words that I give you:

"Mary, in the name of Jesus, will you forgive me for all that I have done to you, the scars I have inflicted on you, the irrational decision I made to terminate your life prematurely? I just did not know what I was doing. The fears, the guilt, the emotions just drove me beside myself. So in the presence of Jesus, the Holy Spirit and our Heavenly Father, and especially in the name of Jesus Who is our Common Creator, our Common Redeemer, and our Common Reward and hopefully the One Whom we will encounter some day. In His name, will you forgive me for what I have done to you? I am sorry. I acknowledge my guilt, and I repent of it, will you forgive me?"

And then I symbolize the child, and I say, "Mommy in the name of Jesus, I accept your request for forgiveness, and I forgive you completely, unconditionally, totally. And I release you

44

from the consequences now and for all eternity, in the name of Jesus, Amen."

Praise You, Jesus, thank you, Jesus.

And then I symbolize the child again and have it address the mother: "Mommy, will you forgive me for all the grief and anguish, panic, confusion I caused by being inside your womb. I just did not know what I was doing, dear mommy. So whatever scars, hurt, anguish that I wrought within you in any dimension, in the name of Jesus, I ask you, will you now forgive me for what I have done to you? I am sorry, mommy, and by the blood, and the death of Jesus and His rising from the dead, will you forgive me?"

And then I tell the mother to speak to the child and forgive it back. "Mary, my child, in the name of Jesus, I accept your request for forgiveness and from my own heart forgive you also, completely, and I release you from the consequences now and forever, Amen."

Praise You, Jesus, thank you, Jesus.

Jesus, You told us whatever you bind on earth shall be bound in heaven, whatever You loosed on earth shall be loosed in heaven. Jesus we claim these words. You are released, Jeannette because we are claiming the words of Jesus. You are forgiven. Now the child is free.

So, thank you, Jesus and praise You, Jesus.

Now the Lord Jesus and Mary — Mary would you take the child now in your arms? And let us go outside to the waiting room where the grandparents are, the parents of Jeannette. Let us accost them.

So Jesus and Mary walk out. There they are. And with Jesus and Mary there, I ask the grandmother of the child to ask its forgiveness and I ask the grandmother, will you say to the child after me these words, "My granddaughter, in the name of Jesus, will you forgive me for the way I talked to my own daughter Jeannette and told her why she should have an abortion? That all the women are doing it these days. I told her, 'Why don't you listen to your doctor, he knows what is best for you.' I also told her, 'You will have a hard time, no man will ever look at you again if you have this child. You are going to jeopardize your whole future, you won't be able to develop and fulfill yourself as a woman.' And you know I gave this daughter of mine so many reasons, and I do feel I persuaded her to come to this type of decision.

"So, little Mary, in the name of Jesus, will you forgive me, your grandmother, for whatever I have done to bring about your premature death? I acknowledge my guilt, and I repent of it, and by the love of Jesus and by the wounds in His hands and His feet, will you forgive me, your grandmother, what I have done to you?"

And then I speak for the child and say, "Yes, granny, in the name of Jesus, I do accept your request and I also now forgive you completely and unconditionally, and I release you now of the consequences on your Judgment Day and for all eternity on the crown of thorns Jesus had on His head. Amen."

Praise You, Jesus, thank you, Jesus. We thank you Jesus. Glory to you Lord, Thank you, Father. Glory to your Holy Spirit.

And, grandfather, will you come over here now, in the presence of Jesus and Mary and the child, and will you ask your granddaughter forgiveness for what you have done? So won't you say after me, "Mary, in the name of our common Savior, will you forgive your grandfather for the way I have taken my daughter aside and told her: 'You just cannot swing it alone economically with this child, why don't you get rid of it? You know this man if he really loved you, he would not have done this to you, so it is not a love child. And you know also, the Church is just making too many demands on us Christians these days. And I do think God Himself understands, and He will excuse you.' And I gave her so many reasons from the darkness of my own mind, so I am guilty in so many ways — collusion — of your premature termination. So in the name of Jesus, will you forgive me of all I have done to you? I am sorry, I repent of it. Will you forgive me?"

Then I speak for the child and say, "Grandpop, in the name of Jesus, I accept your request for forgiveness, and I grant it to you, completely, unconditionally, totally, and I release you from the consequences, now and forever, Amen."

And once this is done, Jesus and Mary walk to the side and with them I am there, and I tell Jesus, "Jesus would you now call your archangels?" By Your dying and rising, You have built a highway from earth to heaven and opened the gates of heaven. I want You to call an archangel and entrust this child who has now been reconciled to all these significant people on earth and has been baptized and now has a right to heaven. Will You call one of your archangels and tell Mary to give the child over to the archangel, and before the angel leaves, will You give this angel the commandment, "Take this child swiftly and securely up the highway to heaven and it is Your command that this child have a seat in one of the highest choirs around the throne of God the Father."

Jesus, You said, "Ask and you shall receive." I ask You, Jesus just this: From the infinite love and goodness of Your heart, and I do know You will hear me.

So praise You, Jesus, thank you, Jesus. Thank you, Mary, for all you have done. Thank you Heavenly Father, and thank you, Holy Spirit. In glory to you now and forever and ever and ever, AMEN.

"I have found this form of healing prayer fantastically releasing to women who have had abortions. Social workers, doctors, psychotherapists have used it and confirmed the fact that it has tremendous releasing and healing powers. And by the Grace of God I do hope it will be used by many, many others for the healing of souls and for the bringing about of the reign of God in our hearts and minds and bodies, of men and women in our nation. So be it, AMEN."

Healing the Self Image

The way to this "healing of souls" of which Father Lazanski spoke can be opened when we forgive others, when others forgive us, and also when we forgive ourselves. Many, many of us are in need of self-forgiveness. Many, many of us in some ways are rejecting of our own selves.

Every person, no matter what the age, has a self-image. He or she believes certain things about him or herself. We tend to filter, separate out, select from all outside stimuli — from family, members of our work places, others in the larger social settings. We form opinions about ourselves from relationships, from events, from our environments. We choose stimuli that are consistent with what we believe to be true about our inner selves.

Often what we hold to be true about ourselves is simply not true at all. Chances are that if I am uncomfortable with myself — if I get easily upset with myself and with others, if I experience sudden and lasting hostilities, frustrations giving rise to inner conflicts, then it is likely I am accepting unfounded values about myself. The discrepancy between perception and reality causes disharmony in my person and puts strains on my relationships with others.

We are born as a center of attraction, and as infants, we make our needs known. As we grow, our needs and wants should develop with a maturity that makes it possible for us to be responsive to the needs and wants of others as well — to allow others to be the centers of attraction when necessary. Such maturation is often hampered by our fear to let go of control that we have over others and the expectations that we construct within ourselves.

Without control, I feel angry because I cannot manipulate, and I cannot accept that others will not live up to the expectations I place upon them.

These expectations feed into my self-created need to control. And now I experience anger, bitterness, conflict, hostility, which turned inward against myself, become depression. I am unhappy. I am a failure. I believe I am unworthy. I have low self-esteem. I have failed to control others. I have failed to be perfect in all things. Therefore, I am no good.

How do I correct this self-image? Let us examine how it was possibly generated. It is created a little at a time. Go back to early childhood. A mother or father will tell the child it has done something bad — you know, "You have taken your sister's doll and thrown it on the floor. It has broken. This action is bad."

Now the child at an early age does not distinguish between his being and the result of his actions. He will feel that he himself is bad. That is a distortion of reality. When reprimanded, he will not hear that what is being said refers to his behavior, but will apply the reprimand to his own personhood. Every time the parent chastises the child for an action which is wrong, inadequate, inappropriate, not acceptable, he will not interpret it in the fullness of the reality which is: your mother and father love you and accept you as a person, but they are labeling what you did as worthy of negative criticism. Mother and father love you so much, as a matter of fact, that they are helping you to adjust to the value system by which the family lives.

So the child, increment by increment, molds these feelings, misrepresented in his imagination, not yet able to apply reason. If we believe negatively about our self image, we begin unconsciously to act out the untruths we believe to be true.

We can renew our belief in ourselves, our images of ourselves, by reflecting on the events of childhood, and this time apply logic to such events. Correct them using your reason, and you may just replace the negative emotions with corresponding feelings of acceptance and love. Destroy the untruth in yourself and replace it with the truth. You are a good person, likable, acceptable. Growing up you were not rejected, but you were surrounded by those who cared for you and about you.

Now you can express these positive feelings; you no longer need to suspect the motivations of others. You can become comfortable with yourself and now with other people. You can now tolerate that other people will differ in opinion. Now when someone speaks to you about an action of yours in a negative way, you can separate the disparagement of that action from the disparagement of your own being. With maturity, you can decide to discuss, accept, dismiss what is being said.

Know that you have a creative mechanism within yourself which can help you achieve your best possible self. That imagination which may have blurred realities can be used to image and then manifest the loving, loved, accepting and accepted person you are now in your new roles. These are necessary conditions to personality transformations.

Regardless of the type of therapy used, a person must see himself in a new role before change can occur. The aim is not to fashion a fictitious self which is all-powerful, arrogant, all-important — that kind of self is as inappropriate and unrealistic as the inferior image of self.

Find the real self.

Mental health professionals constantly deal with persons who short-change themselves. There is no such thing as a superiority complex. People who act that way actually suffer from feelings of inferiority. Their "superior" selves are cover-ups to hide from themselves and from others their deep-rooted feeling of inadequacy and insecurity. If we see ourselves as fear-haunted, anxiety-ridden, defeated nobodies, that is a false picture, and the false must go.

Within you right now is the power to do things you never thought possible. This power comes to you just as soon as you change your belief, just as soon as you dehypnotize yourself from such self-limiting concepts as "I cannot do it, I am unworthy, I do not deserve it." Let us remember that feelings of inferiority originate most often not from the reality of an experience, but from our evaluations of that experience.

Being an inferior tennis player does not make you an inferior person. This distinction is important. We must learn to judge ourselves, measure ourselves, not against the standards and norms of others, but against the standards and norms for ourselves. If we do not do this, we always will be coming out second best.

Also, if illogical reasoning tells us we are unworthy, we do not deserve success and happiness, then we are liable to suppress our talents and our abilities. The truth is, you are not inferior. You are not superior. You are, simply, you. You are unique. You are not in competition with anyone else on the face of this earth because you are an individual. You are not supposed to be like any other person. No person is supposed to be like you.

As you begin to let go of the falsehoods about yourself and as you begin to live the truth of who you are, you are free to get in touch with your own basic goodness. Remember, God created you, as you are, in His likeness and image. This goodness of who you are becomes the foundation of your personality, upon which you build and grow into all that you can be in the eyes of God. Know yourself, your strengths. Rejoice in your giftedness, and especially, rejoice in the giftedness of others.

Know also your weaknesses, and do not be unforgiving of them. Own up to your limitations. They are yours and nobody else's. You will have them until you die. Stop defending yourself and denying those weaknesses. Use that energy, instead, for self-fulfillment.

Accept yourself, and you will find a new calmness, a new collectiveness, a new attitude that is embracing and tolerant of others. Then you can say, "Whatever someone says of me, it is either true, or it is false. If it is true, then why should I be disturbed? It is true. If, on the other hand, if it is false, why should I get upset because, simply, it is not true.

Stop trying to control others, manipulating the lives of others. Cease making expectations for them, and you will have more success in your life. Consequently, you will appreciate who you are. You will be healed and be capable of being a healing person.

A Prayer for Renewing The Self-Image

Father Lazanski offers the following prayerful reflection for the release of a person from self-accusation, condemnation, self-deprecation as a petition to the Holy Spirit to reburnish that person's self-image so that he will discover that he is made to God's image and likeness. I would like to close this chapter with his prayer:

"You are the image of God. You are His son or His daughter. You are from a royal, princely family. You are a prince or a princess. If that truth will just sink in, and that deep self-image is burnished, then you will recover your identity, your uniqueness, your dignity, your personhood, your sanctity. You can be reborn. A second birth takes place. The Holy Spirit has promised that He will reconstruct us, regenerate us, bring us to a new order. And I believe He does this by His creative powers, here and now because of the dying and rising of Jesus. So I claim this type of functioning by Jesus and by the Spirit for the glory of God the Father, AMEN."

Father Albert A Fredette, M.S.

Chapter 4

WHY AM I NOT HEALED?
CAN I, TOO, BE A HEALER?

If we are not healed, why is that? And if we are not administering the healing powers of Jesus unto others, why is that? We must look into our own hearts and minds to discern what obstacles there might be that prevent us both from being healed and from being healing people. A valid question we need to ask ourselves is: Can I, too, be a healer? Can I be the Lord's instrument? Can I be a channel of His power — His healing power, and of His compassionate love?

Of course the answer is "yes," because we are called to do His work. After Jesus ascended into heaven, His Disciples and Apostles did His work because they were called to do the follow-up, and now, in our turn, so are we.

Mark tells us Jesus called His Disciples together and gave them authority to cast out evil spirits, to heal every disease, sickness, without exception and told them to go do it. That is a tall order. It means "touch everyone." Heal the sick, raise the dead, make the lepers clean, drive out evil spirits. Did the Lord invite only His Disciples and Apostles to do this?

Are we listening to His voice? He shows us what to do and how to do it. He has told us we can speak His words of assurance, that if we ask anything in His Name, pray with confidence and trust, then we are to believe we have it. Do we believe that? Are we following Him?

I have asked the Lord in prayer what He calls me to do in following Him. He says, "Well, I am not walking the streets of Southern Pines, or Cape Cod, or the Bronx, or Manila, but you are. So I ask you to do the things you know I did when I walked the streets of Jerusalem." Remember, He said in John 14:12: "He who believes in me will also do the works that I do, and greater works than these will he do."

We need to believe that as Christians committed to the Lord, we are to do His work where we live, in our families, within our towns, cities, states, the world. In my years in the healing ministry — in all the places I have been called — I have witnessed many kinds of healing — healing of cancer, heart disease, broken bones, arthritis, depression, migraine headaches, multiple sclerosis.

Then what stands in the way of us being healed? What stands in the way of us taking care of the living as healing ministers?

We have already explored the importance of unforgiveness as a barrier that must be removed if there is to be healing. We examine now other possible obstacles in our hearts and in our lives that block us from being healed. We consider next what attitudes, what assets we need to develop if we are to seek the gifts from the Holy Spirit that empower us to continue to do the healing work of Jesus Christ here and now.

Obstacles and Blocks to Healing

People come to healing services, and some are healed, and some are not. Among the reasons for not being healed are: (1) selfish prayer (2) unwillingness to let go of what needs to be changed in our lives (3) false humility (4) false pride (5) negative attitudes toward ourself, others and God (6) refusal to accept personal weaknesses and limitations (7) lack of openness to God's will and (8) attaching false values to human suffering.

(1) Selfish prayer

The Lord always answers our prayers — providing they are not selfish. Selfish prayer blocks healing. I will give you an example. I gave a talk in Leominster, Massachusetts to members of Women Aglow International, the Protestant charismatic movement. The president of the group asked me if I would pray over some people. A rather distraught young woman approached me and requested prayers for her husband. "What is wrong with your husband,?" I asked.

She said, "Well he is an alcoholic. He left the children and me and is seeing another woman. I want you to pray to God to change him."

I said, "I bet when he is not drinking, he is a real nice guy." She agreed, adding that he was really kind and generous, gentle and loving.

I told her I could not pray for what she was requesting, because that is asking God to change her husband to the way she wanted him to be. That is control, and control belongs to God, not to her. I told her she could pray for twenty years, and her husband would not change. That prayer makes no sense. Because God is love, and only He can give love, and if we ask for love, we get it — not power to control.

Instead, I offered to pray over her, and I did, and she was overpowered by the Spirit.

She phoned me two days later and said, "Father Al, I have got to tell you what happened after you prayed over me that night. The next day my husband came home, and he said, 'Well, I thought this over, I told the lady it is finished. You are my wife, these are our children. We belong together."

What I had suggested to her when I prayed over her was that "the Lord will change your attitudes, so you will be more loving, and I guaranteed that this would happen, in the name of Jesus Christ, if she agreed to that. We will pray that you will be more kind and accepting of your husband as he is with all the potential for growth and change."

Our attitudes are like a prism — a piece of triangular glass. If we turn it, it catches different rays of sun, and then as we turn it again, the rays change. Every time we change our attitude, we see the world and events and people around us in different ways. So we ask God to change our attitudes to become better persons, better children of the Father in Heaven and better brothers and sisters to the Lord Jesus. If we allow ourselves to be inspired and guided by the Spirit, then our attitudes change, and those around us change. Isn't that wonderful? That is the way it works. That is the power of healing prayer.

(2) Changing ourselves

If you believe that the truth is in Jesus, then you must pursue such changes. You must give up the old attitudes, the old way of life. You must put aside the old self and be renewed to put on the new self which was created in God's way, in goodness and in holiness and in truth.

From St. Paul: "From now on there are to be no more lies, no more deception of self, no more trying to control God, to deceive God. You must speak the truth to one another, to yourself and to the Lord. Since we are all parts of one another, you should not let the sun set on your anger, or you give the devil a foothold. If you are a thief, stop stealing and instead help someone who is in need. Guard against foul talk; let your words be for the improvement of others and do good to your listeners. Otherwise you will only be grieving the Holy Spirit of God who has marked you with His seal for you to be set free when the day comes. Never hold grudges, lose your temper, permit spitefulness and call others ill names. Be friends with one another, and forgiving of one another as readily as God forgave you in Christ."

The key here: lose your old self. Get rid of anything within us that inclines us to things not of the Lord. How do we do that? We get to know ourselves by asking for healing of what is not of the

Lord within us. Then we can see through the eyes of Jesus the way He loves us. When we begin to love ourselves like that, all the things we do not like about ourselves fall away, and we become closer to our larger self which is the image of God. When we touch the spirit of Christ within us, it is like a warm embracing flame, melting all that is ungodly. When we do that we can truly say to others, "I love you." We can love another person only when we can love ourself. We cannot give what we do not have.

(3) False humility

Another reason we may not be healed is false humility. We say, Lord, I am not worthy. Lord, you know I am not worthy. Other people are more important than me.

False humility is insulting to God since He created us in His likeness and image. Remember, it is God's will that we be made whole and holy, and it is the work of Satan to make us believe we are unworthy. Some people say, "Well, the devil doesn't tempt me." I ask, "How do you feel about yourself?" "Well, I feel I am no good." Then I say, "You do not have to have Satan come after you, for you are doing his work already." It is a lie that you are no good. We are created in His image and loved by our Father in heaven.

We are worthy because we have been made worthy by the Precious Blood of Jesus Christ. The conviction that God has no time to bother with you because He has greater things to do for more important people is false and deceitful.

(4) False pride

False pride also interferes with healing. False pride says, I do not need anyone. I can take care of myself. That is false pride, and that is not true. God created us as social beings. We need to be interdependent, not dependent upon one another, but interdependent.

We all have something to give to the Body of Christ, and we are members of that Body. We all have responsibilities to that Body. But we also have the right to take from the Body of Christ when we are the person in need. If we accept the Holy Mystical Body of Christ and our membership in it, then there is no room for false pride in our life.

We need to eliminate our fear of reaching out, we need to touch one another. There was a film done in Berkeley, California based on an experiment in touch as a healing element. It was done in a hospital setting. Nurses who were well-balanced and loving people were selected and told to touch patients in a loving way as they worked. Another group, the nurses who approached their work as just a job, were not so instructed.

At the end of the project the hemoglobin count was ordered for all the patients in the research. Those who had been shown care and concern and a loving touch had increased hemoglobin counts. Those who were not so ministered to did not show any sign of change.

(5) Negative attitudes spread

All negative attitudes can serve as blocks — negative attitudes toward ourself, others, and toward God. Again, they are the work of Satan, and they can have physical effects. Telling your deepest self that you are no good sends the message — a message of doom — throughout your body, your spirit, your emotions. You can condemn your body to be ill. We need to take authority in the name of Jesus Christ over our own body and cells and command them to do the work and be submissive to do the work that they were created to do.

The white cells are there to bring healing to the other cells. In conjunction with medical experts, we need to take authority over our bodies and do everything possible for us to be well. We need to manage our wellness, not say we are not feeling well.

By the way, how are you living? What is your lifestyle? Do you stay up until 2 a.m., overeat, fail to exercise? Then you are not taking charge, and you are going to be sick. Being awake to and aware of the healing presence of God in our lives does not give us license to lose command over our bodies, to abandon the ordinary and natural means of healing. Anointed medicine has healing power.

I recall a doctor telling me he was going to take himself off the case of a man who was on dialysis for his kidneys because he was not following doctor's orders, ignoring the diet regulations. But at the same time this patient was disregarding his physician's instruction, he was having members of his prayer group coming into the hospital room to pray over him. This same man later came to one of my workshops, and I confronted him, saying "If you do not scrupulously follow your doctor's orders, I will ask people not to pray over you."

We should thank the Lord for our medical professionals, for the talent He has given them, and we should utilize to the full extent of our need the expertise of these men and women. We should acknowledge our illnesses, seek assistance that we need from medical personnel and anoint all that they do with prayer. When we do that, wonderful things happen — healings of all kinds take place. Nothing is too great for God.

At St. Vincent's Medical Center in Toledo, Ohio, I introduced prayer to the doctors and nurses and the staff of 2,600 became aware that prayer indeed has a place in a hospital. I started organizing workshops on the power of healing prayer to introduce the medical people to the concept of healing through the power of Jesus Christ. All the work of the medical experts is done through the power of Christ, but sometimes the staff does not know that.

So what happened at St. Vincent's through prayer is what you might expect: all kinds of people were healed in all kinds of ways that the doctors themselves could not explain. For example, there was a nurse named Jenny, who was a float nurse — a nurse who moves from crisis to crisis. One day, as she was rushing to answer a call, she noticed a man in his hospital room, and something within her told her she had better stop. So she asked him how he was doing. He told her he had a heart problem, an occluded artery, and in his case surgery would be difficult. There was nothing to be done and the doctor could not predict how long he would live in his condition.

Jenny asked the patient if he had any children. He said, "Yes." She said he should be home with them, and he said he would love that. She asked if he believed in prayer. (Everyone in a hospital bed believes in prayer). So she prayed over him briefly and left. On the way back from the crisis, she saw his doctor looking at an x-ray and shaking his head. She asked him what was wrong. He told her that his patient — it was the man she had prayed over — had an occluded artery, one hundred percent blocked, and he had taken another x-ray, and now it was one hundred percent open.

She asked, "Would you say something extraordinary has happened"? He replied, "Yes, and I would like to know what." And she went quietly on her way, not saying any more because she was not sure he was ready to hear it.

How do we anoint what the doctors do? At the medical center I assigned one of the sisters to the pre-op area, and she prayed with people who wanted prayer prior to surgery. What she saw happening was the elimination or significant reduction of fear, anxiety, tension and stress. When the surgeon arrived, he found his task easier and the anesthesiologist began to see it was taking less anesthesia. In the recovery room, the time was also shortened.

The process of healing was being quickened because prayer was part of it. Negative attitudes which do not respect and anoint medical practices certainly impede the process of healing.

Negative attitudes may be seen also as demanding a sign from God. "Okay, God, if you show me, then I will believe." For people like this I have found that even if someone were raised from the dead, they still would not believe because they are blinded. They are in a cocoon of darkness and they cannot see the light. They demand a sign from God.

The negative attitudes toward others, of course, involves an area we have already discussed in depth: the feelings we harbor when we do not forgive: anger, retaliation, jealousy, bitterness, rage, frustration, and even hatred.

(6) Rejection of our limitations

We cannot be healed if we refuse to accept our personal weaknesses and limitations. We like to deny we are ill. We fight ourselves.

Or we might deny that we tend to lose patience or are quick to anger. We do not own up to being that kind of person. Maybe we are people who go into rages for no reason. We do not own up to that. Instead we say we will pray and ask God to take the behavior away. We have limitations and weaknesses, and they are ours, and we are going to have them until we die. So every time we say we are going to try doing our best, we probably fail because we first did not own up to our weaknesses.

Instead, I would suggest, in terms of healing, to stand before the Lord in humility and honesty. Identify your bad habits and recognize that you are the person who has them. Then tell the Lord you are not going to try any more. But turn to Him, recognize your failings and invite Him into them. Ask Him to transform them into strengths, that you might accomplish things clearly beyond your ability, and then express your gratitude to God.

In order for you to learn the truth which sets you free, you have to believe that without Christ, you can do nothing. If you acknowledge you are not perfect, in the spirit of love and submission, then the Lord will listen to your prayer, because it is not a selfish prayer. It is a prayer for a change of attitude, perhaps to be more giving, more gentle, more caring, more forgiving, more loving. You are asking to become a better Christian, and that prayer will be answered. It is not a controlling prayer, but an invitation to the Lord to enter our brokenness, to make us more loving. The loving person is the healed and healing person.

Our need to be perfect is a false assumption, as is a compulsion to be loved by everyone. Talk about setting yourself up for a fall! Living out such false assumptions invites failure. They cannot be realized.

(7) Denying God's will

If we are not open to God's will, we cannot be healed; we cannot be healers. His will is for us to be made whole and holy. But maybe we want our will to prevail. We schedule God. We tell Him what we want Him to do and when we want Him to do it. We tell Him what we need and how to heal us.

The control God has given us is free will. We can choose. The Lord respects our decision. What happens is, He just stays there, and He lets us go on, in our own design, and then we fall flat on our face. And then we come back, saying, "Why did you abandon me? How much must I pray before you hear me? How come you are so distant from me, God?"

But we forgot that He never moved. We are the ones who turned away and walked away. That is what we do. We tell Him what to do, how to heal us. When we do that, there is no way we can be healed or become healers. We need to let that go. Let God be the one to show us the way.

And if we lack commitment to Christ, a strong commitment, then we are complacent Christians, neither hot nor cold. Either we drop the title of Christians because we are not living it, or we commit ourselves to Christ and bring orientation and meaning to our lives. We need a strong commitment to life, the life that is Jesus in us.

(8) Attaching false values to human suffering

Another barrier to healing is attaching false values to human suffering. Sometimes we assign to personal trials a distraught interpretation of the cross in our life. How many times have you gone to hospitals and heard ill people say that God is punishing them for their sins? How can total love be punishing? Impossible.

The only thing God can give us is love. His love. So to say He is being punitive is a gross misinterpretation of the cross in our life. We do not see that sometimes we are on the suffering side of the cross, and that is only a temporary occurrence. We can offer up those sufferings in the name of the Lord. The other side of the cross is the sunshine side. We need to resurrect from our suffering, and we do so once we offer up to the Lord and embrace His Cross with our suffering so that it becomes redemptive.

The Unknown Reason

Sometimes you just do not know why a person is not healed. In the Province of San Mateo in the Philippines, during my trip there in 1991 there was a little girl named Isabella. She had a skin problem, and she was not healed, and I simply did not know why. There seemed to be no reason, nice little girl like that. She should have been healed. I said to those gathered at the healing service, "If this was your little girl, you would want us all to pray for her, so let us do that." They did, and I took her on my lap, and felt the compassion the Lord would have felt for children like that, and I loved her. And she was the only one at that service not healed.

I had done a couple of healing services in Santiago, Philippines in 1979, but the results were not nearly as extraordinary as what happened when I returned in 1991. In some places, for example in the village of Tahanan, south of Manila, every single person who came up to the prayer teams was healed. There was just endless applauding and incredible healings. There was one woman who asked that a huge lump on her breast be prayed over, so I asked a woman on a prayer team to put her hand there, and it was a huge tumor. We prayed, and asked her what happened, and she said, "It is gone." At one service there were about 5,000 people, standing room only.

Why was that one little girl not healed? I do not know. Perhaps the healing came later. Why, on the other hand, were so many, many others healed so instantaneously in the Philippines? I think because they were poor and could not afford doctors; and because despite the calamities of their country, they maintained a joyful and stead-fast devotion to Our Blessed Mother. Maybe the other factor was that despite my exhaustion, I had compassion for them, with all the people praying together, united as a community of faith, and this combination spells victory.

Set Yourselves Free

To be healed, we need to be set free. All the blocks we have discussed are obstacles to being healed. Recognize them as they pertain to you. Healing begins in the deepest part of who we are, our very self, made to God's likeness and image. We are temples of the Holy Spirit. Instead of calling for God out there, get in touch with His presence in our hearts. What a big difference it would make in our lives if every time we were tempted to gossip, or to sin in any way, we would, instead, kindle our awareness that God the Father has placed the spirit of Christ in our hearts. This fact should revolutionize our whole life. This should be a spiritual revolution, as St. Paul calls it.

I recall a woman sharing with others at a healing workshop a healing she experienced while being prayed for, and she used those exact words to express her impression of what happened. She said, "I was set free."

She said, "No matter where I am, even when I am with people who love me, I feel I do not belong unless I am serving. Even at prayer meetings, I have to be busy, busy, busy. But today, when I was prayed over, one of the women said that as she was praying she pictured me at the age of seven or eight. She saw me with my hands down at my side, very forlorn, in a very dismal place. When she told me that, I could not picture that place, and then I realized that place was inside of me. I thought about one day when I was little standing in my backyard and feeling so very much alone. I was the last of fourteen children. Then I felt I was inside looking out of my body to a place I did not know. I felt the loneliness leave me, come right out of my body through my feet, and I was filled with joy. Praise the Lord. I had a tremendous inner healing, long overdue. I was set free."

So what are the obstacles within yourself that are preventing your freedom? What are my obstacles? How are you and I going to identify them? And once we identify them, what will we do with them? Christ has redeemed us. He is victorious over sin, temptation, death, disease, pain, brokenness and the wiles of the devil. The devil lost the battle. He has not finished working, but he has lost the final battle.

Illness is within us. Jesus mentioned how evil comes from within the heart of man. It is not what goes into a person, but what comes out of a person. When there is lack of balance and harmony in our spirits and emotions, then our body is affected in a negative way. That is why praying over symptoms does not work; but probing deeper often locates a psychological, emotional, spiritual problem that needs to be resolved.

Healing begins from within and moves outward to encompass the spirit, the emotions and the body. If the illness is lodged in our spirit, then our emotions are affected, and our body weakens. We need to recognize this interaction of spirit, emotions and physical being, and seek to identify what it is that imprisons us in illness.

Francis MacNutt has said that physical healing is actually the least of healings, because healing begins in the recesses of who we are. It is spiritual radiation coming forth, moving through the psyche and the emotions and then to the physical being, so that the total person will be healed. Healing radiates from the very core of the personality, penetrating layer upon layer.

Perhaps we need to pray to become free enough to be healed, and then we need to protect ourselves after being healed, so as not to lose the healing the Lord has granted us. Then, with a deep sense of gratitude, we need to praise God and give Him thanks:

Eternal Father, we are gathered today to raise our voices and hearts to give You praise, adoration, worship and thanksgiving. We approach Your throne with confidence, knowing that as Your children, we are loved by You. We come to You seeking new gifts, new blessings and more graces. We ask You in the name of Jesus, Your Son and Our Lord, the gifts from the Holy Spirit; first, the gift of openness, that we may want to hear Your Word, and hearing Your Word, we may desire to live it fully, and that living Your Word fully, we may witness to it among Your people, bringing peace, joy and happiness to all, and gratitude to You, our Father, in heaven. We ask You for the gifts of knowledge and learning, that we may know Jesus more intimately and learn the way to holiness through Him. We also ask for the gifts of humility, gentleness, and simplicity of heart, that we may learn not to boast in the name of achievements, but as children, to rejoice in the gifts of one another, and the love of God. We make this prayer through Christ Our Lord. AMEN

Can I, Too, Be A Healer?

There is a season for everything, a time for every occupation under heaven. What time is it for you today? Today is a time for healing. A time for you to learn how the Lord wants to channel His healing power through you. He said to us, "Come, follow me," and all you readers, regardless of age, who are interested in gaining power, real power through Him, are invited. As human beings we seek power to control persons and things, and sometimes we seek the power at the wrong source, falling prey to powers not of God. If we seek power and control with Satan and demons, we are courting deception, falsehood and destruction. Jesus is the only source of power and true love. The power and compassionate love of Jesus are good. Evil is that which is lacking life, which is incomplete, and in need of healing. We need Christ's power to bring others to health, to life and wholeness, which is accomplished through us as conduits, through us as healing people in His name.

"May the God of Strength be with you, holding you in a strong-fingered hand. May you be the sacrament of His strength to those whose hands you hold. May the blessing of strength be with you."

There are certain qualities that define healing people. One of my pastoral education students at St. Vincent's Medical Center, a nun from Gary, Indiana, sent me a letter which included prayers for these qualities which I share with you. The first thing we need to be healers is strength. We need to take care of ourselves if we are going to minister. We need a strong heart. God wants us to be well ourselves if we are to be healers.

Healing ministry can be as draining emotionally and mentally, as it is physically. Brother Armand Binette, a La Salette brother who is also in the healing ministry, says that during the times you have negative attitudes you should not pray over anyone. He backs off praying over people if he feels that he does not have himself in order. And you must not allow yourself, when praying over other people, to be overcome by negatives you may be feeling in association with their afflictions. It is wonderful to feel sad and hurt for them, and of course, to feel compassion, but you need to focus on the positive. As Brother Binette points out, "When you are praying for people, even people who might not be present, you need to picture them as being healed, picture them as being whole and doing the things they should be doing. If the leg is affected, maybe picture the person getting up and dancing and feeling wonderful."

As well as physical and psychic stamina, we need spiritual strength, the strength of increased faith. I like to think of faith as a gift from God that we can use or abuse, but never lose. When someone says he has lost his faith, I believe he did not lose it, but he abused it. God does not give us the gift and then take it back. Faith in the healing ministry is built on experience — the experience of God in our life, the experience of God working through us — and it increases as you see people healed, and as you are a part of that. Confidence in your prayer increases. Remember even though we are unworthy — as expressed in the prayer before Communion — through God's Word we become worthy.

God always initiates the dialogue in terms of prayer. We may desire to pray, wish, need and want to pray, but it is always God who initiates that wish to give Him glory. It is through such dialogue that our faith can grow and be demonstrated.

In Luke 18: 35-43, there is an example of God prompting this dialogue and bringing someone to healing. There was a blind man sitting on the side of the road, at the entrance to Jericho, begging, when he heard the noise of the crowd. It was God initiating a dialogue with the blind beggar. When he heard those crowds, that was God beginning the conversation, that was the Lord speaking to him. The blind man responded by asking what was going on, and they told him that Jesus was passing by, so he called out, "Jesus, Son of David, have pity on me." Now it is interesting that the people in front of Jesus were the leaders in the community, the superiors. They scolded the blind man and told him to be quiet.

Consider the parallel in your churches, communities, families — here is someone in need of healing, and the people chosen by God Himself to be out front tell this person in need to be quiet. Isn't that strange? But the blind man shouted all the louder — "Jesus, Son of David, have pity on me." Jesus stopped and ordered those out front to bring this man to him. See how He uses authority? He told the leaders what to do. When the blind man came Jesus asked what he wanted done for him — therein the dialogue — bringing together the needy and He who fulfills the need. He replied, "Let me see again," indicating he was not blind from birth. Jesus said, "Receive your sight, your faith has saved you." Instantly his sight was restored and he followed Jesus, praising God — that was his response for restoration of his sight — he praised and followed God. All those who saw praised God also.

We see in this incident a teaching on healing prayer. There is the Lord who is filled with authority, and the beggar, who represents us. There is a dialogue. Always in the healing ministry there is dialogue between the person ministering and the one being ministered to — dialogue through the Lord.

"May the God of Gentleness be with you, caressing you with sunlight, rain and wind. May His tenderness shine through you to warm you and all who are hurting."

If you meet people in the healing ministry who are not gentle, you know it immediately. They take authority where they do not have it; they shout. The Lord was strong, and the Lord was gentle. He is our model. We need to develop gentleness within ourselves. We need to develop the same kind of empathy and compassion that the Lord had for people who were broken. So, too, as we are broken, we need to look upon others who are broken and approach them gently. We are healed and healing through gentleness, not through violence and arrogance.

Remember that the person who is seeking healing is in pain and hurting. Express to them with kindness and gentleness that you are in touch with their suffering, that you want to help and see them restored. Loud prayers are very disturbing.

I had a dream once. I was on an airplane, and I was looking for a slot though which to mail an envelope, but I could not find one. Finally I found a little place, and when I pushed the envelope through, I followed it and found myself free-falling to earth. I said to myself in the dream, "I wonder if God can hear me if I whisper?" So I said "Help" in a whisper. Do you know what happened? It was like a skywriting plane had put the word in big letters, and the words filled the sky, and I experienced the deepest sense of peace, because I knew the Lord heard and I was safe. My Father in heaven had heard the gently whispered cry of His child in distress and answered the prayer.

"May the God of Mercy be with you, forgiving you, beckoning you, encouraging you to say, 'Now I will get up again and go

to my Father's house.' May your readiness to forgive calm the fears and deepen the trusts of those who have hurt you. May the blessing of mercy be on you."

We have all experienced mercy from God. We have all, hopefully, experienced forgiveness from people we have hurt. We need to be merciful. In the previous chapter I stressed how central forgiveness is to the healing proccss. We cannot be healers if we are unforgiving, if we lack mercy and compassion.

"May the God of Wonder be with you, delighting you with thunder, birdsong, sunrise, enchanting your sense, filling your heart, giving you wide open eyes for seeing the splendor in the humble and the majestic. May you open the eyes and the hands, the hearts of the blind and the deaf. May the blessing of wonder be upon you."

Part of being a healer is looking through the Lord's eyes. What the Lord saw was what His Father created — the world, the waters, the birds and flowers. As a little child delights in such things, he develops within himself the spirit of wonder. We need to approach God's healing with wonder: His relationship with us, His working through us for the people He wants healed. We need to be open to that, to approach it with simplicity and acknowledge there is a mystery to all this — an element of wonder, of awe, that we cannot touch.

"May the God of Simplicity be with you, opening you to a clear vision of what is real and true, leading you deeply into the mystery of childhood. And may your dealing with others be marked by honesty which is simplicity, May the blessing of simplicity be upon you."

Related to wonder and gentleness is simplicity. The Lord has called us to be like little children. The quality of simplicity allows us a clear vision, unobstructed by prejudices, whereby we can see the Lord working in our lives.

The quality of simplicity is important in praying for the sick. If you have goodwill, if you are a compassionate channel for the healing power of Jesus Christ, that is the best asset you have. You do not need formulas for prayer. Again, you do not need finely-formed sentences, and you certainly do not need to shout. Stay away from those formulas as if they were magic. There is no magic in relating to God, there is no magic in prayer. Be yourself, just be yourself. If you are confused about who you are, it is very difficult for you to present yourself to the Lord in prayer. If you know who you are, you are in touch with your goodness, and you are sure that God loves you. Love yourself so you can love others.

Go before the Lord in simplicity; let the Spirit guide you in honest and simple prayer. Sometimes the prayer can be silent. Sometimes people do not want to see you praying, so you can say a silent prayer that the Lord will touch them somehow. This is called being a "participative presence." You are there, but you are not doing or saying anything. You are just, simply, "being" to that person. Somehow, in those relationships, something does happen. The person who is likely to resist and be hostile somehow is touched by your concern for them, and they become open to the workings of the Holy Spirit. They become open to healing prayer and open to you as a channel of God's Grace.

The Story of Kim Francis

Following is the story of Kim Francis, 23, who is employed as a nurse in Pawtucket, Rhode Island. Her healing occurred when she was 16 years old, and is an example of praying through "participatory presence." Fr. Fredette tells what happened from his vantage point, and Miss Francis and her mother, Lynn, relate the experience in their own words:

Fr. Fredette: "One day at the La Salette Shrine in Attleboro I got a call from Fr. Joe Ross who is director of youth ministry there. He related that a 16-year-old girl in his group was in the hospital, severely burned from over exposure to a sunlamp and in terrible pain. She could hardly speak because of the pain. He asked me to go pray over her.

I went to the hospital into her semi-private room, where a visitor was with the other patient. I asked her, 'Do you want me to pray over you to get rid of the pain?' I was not surprised when she said, 'Well, Father it is embarrassing.' She was a sensitive teenager, and others were present, and I understood. So I told her not to worry, and I stood silently, my back to the others so they would not know what was going on. I just raised my hand and asked the Lord to relieve her pain. Can you imagine how painful it is to be burnt?"

The Patient, Kim Francis: "I remember I was a high school sophomore at the time, and I believe some of the burns I had were third-degree. I had stayed too long under the lamp. I was in so much pain. It was truly horrible. At the hospital there was talk by the doctors of skin grafts. My face was swollen and the skin cracked.

Then Father Al came to the hospital and prayed over me. It seemed like only seconds. Then I slept through the night, not having previously been able to sleep. There was no pain that night. The next morning I got up, and my face was back to normal. It was unbelievable. All the skin that had been burned was back to normal. I ran around the room I was so happy. I called my mother. The doctors told her it was a miracle. There are no scars on my face."

The Mother, Lynn Francis: "The morning Kim had the burns was the morning my younger daughter was making her First Communion. I took some sterile precautions, and then took her to our pediatrician who advised us to go to an emergency room. There she was met by a surgeon she knew who had previously treated her. He took one look at her and turned around. I could see he was crying. The swelling was so bad. There were second and third degree burns. The swelling was so severe, her lips so distorted that her face was grotesque. I almost passed out looking at her.

I did not know until later that the doctors were discussing skin grafts with her. The next morning when she called from the hospital and told me she was fine I thought, 'Well she has either lost it, or drugs have affected her.' I did not know Father Al had prayed over her. I really thought she had gone off the deep end.

I jumped into the car and raced to the hospital. I looked at her and could not believe what I saw. Her skin was like that of a newborn. She was discharged either that day or the day following. I told her doctor about Father Al. I asked him, 'What do you think?' He said, 'There is no other way that healing was possible. It is God's doing.' Now this doctor is a very compassionate man. He previously had stood beside the bed of my dying daughter and cried. But at the same time he is very down to earth. He is not the kind of person who would say there is a spiritual cause if there could be a medical explanation.

If ever I had doubted that God was with me, it was washed away the day I saw Kim's face healed. I knew He was there. I said to myself, 'I am here, and He was there.' Even when I am overwhelmed by things and start to doubt about God's presence whether He is here, I remember that day and I say, 'He is here.'"

"May the God of Compassion be with you, holding you close when you are weary and hurt and alone, when there is rain in your heart. May you be the warm hand and the warm eyes of compassion for your friends when they reach out to you in need. May the blessing of compassion be upon you."

The Lord was working in the life of Kim Francis to completely restore her, to heal her scars and wipe away all blemishes the burn had caused her. The Lord has compassion for us when we are in need.

As healers we must be compassionate. Compassion means we are with that person who is hurting, we are feeling for that person who is in pain. The Lord took pity for the sheep without a shepherd. The Lord had empathy. Compassion is an aspect of love. To be a healer, we need to be like a reservoir of love. We need to be filled with God's love. We need to keep that reservoir filled, so that only that which spills over will be the work of God and will touch others in a healing way.

Compassion is not the gift of any age group, but it is present wherever, in a community of faith, there is someone hurting. For example, at a La Salette parish in Windsor, Ontario, Canada, we saw that attendance was diminishing, and one day we sat down and said, "What will we do"? Since healing brings life, we decided we would talk about healing to the parishioners at a weekend service. On the feast of the Holy Rosary, the first praying over people was initiated after the Saturday Mass, and this was repeated for some weeks.

I was assigned to celebrate Mass at the chapel of the parish school where elderly people and families generally came because there are no steps to climb. But the praying for healing was occurring only at the main church. One day I said to the people, "I would be really angry if I were you, because at the main church they have this healing prayer every Saturday, and you do not have it here." After Mass I offered to pray with others, with anyone experiencing pain.

A woman came up to me and said, "Father Al, I am in pain. I have had migraine headaches for twenty years, and I cannot even do a day's work."

So I called some young people over, mostly teenagers, and I said, "Gather around our sister who is hurting." About ten of them came. And I said, "Does everyone here love our sister, because if you do not love her, you cannot pray over her. You have to love her." They said, "Yes, we love her." So we prayed over her, and she left, and we left. A few weeks later, the same woman was there after Mass. She said, "Father, you know what happened? After you and the kids prayed over me, I went home, and my migraines were lifted, and I have not had a headache since. I am now doing my work each day with joy."

"May the God of Patience be with you, waiting for you with outstretched arms, letting you find out for yourselves. May His patience with all the young who fall from small heights and the old who fall from greater heights be your patience. May the blessing of patience be upon you."

One thing we have all experienced as we pray over people is the need for a great deal of patience. We have to take time to develop an attitude that there is no rush. You do not have to get all these prayers done, hurry up, fast. One man once told me he could pray one hundred and sixty words per minute. He was a priest. Some people are just like that.

In the healing ministry, you do not have to hurry. One thing about the Lord. He did a lot of work, had a busy schedule. He did not sleep much. Crowds were there waiting. But He had patience. Nowhere in the Gospels does it mention that the Lord ran or rushed. In fact, one time He rode a donkey. No rush.

You have to let the person who is coming to you for healing breathe with you, so you can listen to the meaning of who he is. You have to be open to the Word of God and, for that, you have to pray for the gift of openness. Patience needs to be practiced with self and with others to allow God to be the one who leads. We live in an age of quick solutions and throw aways.

Sometimes people seeking help will seemingly want to talk endlessly, or maybe not communicate at all, being lost, embarrassed and confused. What I do in my counseling mode is pray silently for them and I say, "Lord, love him or her right now." A healing attitude is a listening attitude. You need to listen not only to the words that are said, but also to what those words are conveying, the deeper problems, the ones which must be prayed for. Get to the source, for when the Lord touches the source, the problem is totally resolved.

Sometimes in prayer groups people pray over those who want healing, and they pray only once and then give up. That is not what we are called to do. Even the saints when they felt that God would delay in answering their prayers, would redouble their prayers and persevere. Praying for a person once and dismissing him is not Christian. It is often through praying with perseverance that enlightenment comes, either to the person being prayed over or to the person doing the praying.

We should not abandon our brothers and sisters to unhealed states. When you pray over people, I urge you to persevere until healing takes place. It is not that the Lord is shortchanging us, or that somehow our prayer is imperfect. Perhaps the person has a block, and if we pray again it will surface, and we can call it to the person's attention and address it, and they can become free enough to be healed.

"May the God of Peace be with you, filling the heart that hammers with fear and doubt and confusion. May your peace, the warm mantle of your peace, cover those who are troubled and anxious. May the blessing of peace be on you."

AND:

"May the God of Joy be with you, thrilling you with His nearness, filling your heart to fullness, and filling your throat to wringing, singing exaltations. May the blessing of joy be on you."

We cannot enjoy peace until we get in touch with our own goodness. Peace and joy are fruits of the Holy Spirit. We know the source of healing through its fruit. That is, Satan heals, but it is a fake and deceptive healing. The fruits of being healed through the compassionate love of Christ are, quite simply, peace and joy.

If we have no joy, we are not truly alive. We need to ask the Holy Spirit for that gift so we can seek the joyful aspects of creation, the joyful aspects of those we meet, the joys of life itself.

It is hard to feel joy when one is in great pain. Once in San Francisco, when I was praying with a very powerful prayer group there, a young man came up to me. He had an awful pallor; no life in his eyes or face. He told me that cancer was doing a job on him, sapping all his energy, eating him up. I asked him what he wanted us to pray for, although it may seem obvious, I always ask. It is important to ask what a person wants prayed about because it may not always be the obvious. The young man responded, "I want to get well again."

So we addressed the cancer: "Cancer cells, you have no business being in our brother. He is a child of God, and God does not want him to be sick. Cancer cells, I command you in the Name of Jesus Christ to get out. You are not being obedient to the will of God who created you to serve the body."

As we were praying over him, we could see the blood come back to his cheeks, the clarity returned to his eyes, and he was being healed right before us. And he had a terrible pain. We prayed for the pain to be lifted, and the pain left him. This indicates the need to continue praying. The Lord was present, and the Holy Spirit was there, the Giver of Life. The Holy Spirit was giving life to this young man who, according to the medical field, was dying. He regained his composure, his strength, and he showed joy. He was a happy man. There was a healing and restoration to physical health.

Sometimes pain can prevent persons from doing tasks that bring them joy. At a healing service in Braintree, Massachusetts, I asked whether anyone was in pain, and among those raising their hands was a woman who said she had crippling arthritis in her hands. Her hands were knotted with extreme pain. She said she experienced pain twenty-four hours a day. She asked to be prayed over. Her daughter was standing next to her, and when I began praying over this woman, the daughter turned her back. Well, it was her choice. When I finished praying, I asked if there were any change, and she did not say a word but held out her hand in a fist. I did not understand. But her daughter turned around, looked at her and began to cry. The woman said, "I could never do that before."

It was when she made a fist that the daughter realized that the Lord had entered into this situation, had healed her mother, not only of the pain, but had restored mobility to the hands.

That illustrated the two movements to healing: first you pray that the pain be lifted, and then you continue to pray that movement be restored to the part affected. Finally, the healing is complete. Can you imagine trying to cope every day with gnarled fingers? She had been deprived of doing things she had taken great joy in doing, and joy was restored with the new mobility.

Some people need a kind of healing of feelings directly, giving joy where there once was despair. I remember being at Otis Air Force Base on Cape Cod saying a Mass and offering to pray over people after the liturgy. One woman came forward and said, "I have a teenage daughter who feels she has been rejected both before and after birth. She is always thinking about destroying herself, talking about suicide, can you pray over her?" I invited gathered people to pray for their sister. We prayed that depression, anger and self-rejection be lifted. When I returned another Sunday her mother told me, "You will not believe this, but my daughter is a totally different person. She is now starting to experience joy in her life."

We have reported above a physical healing in Canada, a healing of emotions in Massachusetts — through the compassionate love of Christ, bringing joy where there was pain and self-loathing. We need to remember about emotional healing that there is still a scar left within the person, and this scar can be opened up again when there is new pain and hurt. The person healed needs to keep working on building up self-confidence and self-esteem — for the only full healing occurs, of course, in death itself, and we are not there yet. But getting close and closer in touch with self-goodness is important.

Once we know who we are, we know we are loved by the Father. And one word which encapsulates all this (strength, gentleness, mercy and wonder, compassion, simplicity, patience and peace) — is love. Love is forgiveness; love is prayer; love is acceptance of others. Love needs to be the center of who we are. Love is the kind of gift, that once we experience it, we may want to build a little fence around it, hold on to it tightly. But if we do that, we soon realize we hold nothing. For the nature of love is that for it to grow, and to grow, it has to be shared:

"May the God of Love be with you, listening to you, telling you His secrets, giving Himself to you, drawing you close as you tremble at the edge of self. May His love in you light fires of faith and hope. May these fires grow and burn and burst and inflame the earth. May His love in you glow in your eye. May His love glow in the eyes of your friends. May the blessing of love, the blessing of friendship be upon you."

We are on earth not so much to give as to receive, and once we receive, we share, and that sharing is love. We may ask ourselves how we can be instruments for God's healing, when we need so desperately to be healed ourselves. Jesus calls each one of us to be minister of His love on earth, and St. Paul tells us that Christ has entrusted the message of reconciliation to us. If we waited to be fully healed, we would have to wait until we died. Reach out with the heart of Jesus; our own hearts are so lifeless. We are not called to be saviors or perfect models of peace, for only Jesus is that.

Our own woundedness identifies us with all others who are broken human beings. We are all brothers and sisters, and this very weakness of our wounds becomes our strength. It is through our weaknesses that the Lord works best, where His power and authority and mercy are most manifest. As soon as we recognize we can do nothing without Christ, then it is that we who are strengthened become aware that the Father has placed within our heart the Spirit of Christ.

We make contact with our brother in our weakness, for how else can human contact be made? In our unhealed state our hope is to know Jesus personally. Do you hear the voice of Jesus in your life? Are you relying on Him totally to empower you? Are you in total surrender to Him? If not, how do you get there?

I will tell you how I got there. I asked myself, "What does it take, Lord, for me to commit myself to You one hundred percent? Whenever I ask the Lord for an answer, it usually takes three months — it takes me a long time to figure it out. Well three months after I asked — and I would ask Him every day, saying, "You said You would reveal all things, and I am holding You to Your word" — three months later He revealed the answer in a strange place.

I had taken my pastoral education students to Cedar Point in Ohio, a large fun park. There the Lord chose to answer my request. I was sitting in a gondola, and I looked up and saw the cable holding it. And I said to myself, "Al, if that cable broke, is there anything you could do"? The answer was, absolutely nothing. It took that incident to see myself completely helpless and completely needing the Lord. At that point I committed myself one hundred percent to the Lord.

That is how it needs to be in the healing ministry. We need to empty ourself so that nothing is left, nothing negative—no pride. We need to own up to our weaknesses, and say, "Lord I am that person who has these weaknesses." I can do nothing to change one single cell in a sick person's body — but if it is shared power and authority from the Lord, if, as wounded people we empty ourselves, inviting Him into our attitude, spirit and emotions, then we are guided by the Spirit. As we pray over someone, the Spirit will talk to the Father on behalf of our brother or sister who needs healing.

And the bonus of all this is, as we pray for others, we are healed ourselves. We have to commit ourselves solely and totally to Jesus Christ, our Savior and Redeemer. In the words of St. Paul, it is when we are powerless that we are strong. It is draining to be in the healing ministry, although I have to realize that we are really in the healing ministry from the time we are ordained. Look, the Lord used to run away from crowds, and yet they would advance on Him, and He would take pity on them, and as He did he taught them that the Father in heaven is the Father of love. As He is here, and as we are in Him, we are in the Father.

The Church is, indeed, powerless and relatively ineffectual in a world fraught with evil. We ask ourselves, why then, is the world immersed in evil if life overcame death? How can Jesus Christ have been entrusted to His Body, the Church, and the Church, then, not have much power?

But the power is also within us as individual members of that Body, and perhaps it is that we have not yet accepted the words of Jesus, the Healer, Jesus Who loves us and gives healing power to His Church. We are members of the Mystical Body, and we have the duty, the responsibility, the privilege to pray for one another in a healing way.

We may be called upon to exercise this responsibility when we least expect it, not always at planned healing services, or not always being specifically requested to do so. For example, one day I walked into a place of business in Plymouth, Massachusetts and asked the woman behind the counter to xerox some materials for me that I needed for this book. Her hand and arm were bandaged, and she was struggling to use the word processor. I asked her what happened to her hand. She said, "I burned it last night, spilled some boiling water.' I asked her if it was painful. She said, "Oh, yes, very painful." I took her hand gently and prayed over the pain. I asked then how she felt, whether there was any pain left. She said, "It feels very warm." Usually when there is warmth or tears it is a sign of something going on internally or externally, some kind of healing.

She said she would xerox the pages, and I could pick them up later. When I returned I asked her how her injury was. She said, "The pain is gone." In fact, she changed her mind about going to an emergency room for treatment. Several weeks later she showed this book's editor the injured area of her hand and arm, where the skin was not only healed, but had been regenerated as smooth as a baby's skin.

What wonderful things the Lord does for those who love Him!

HIS POWER IS AMONG US

Chapter 5

THE HEALING MINISTRY: A MYSTERY, NOT MAGIC

I have given many workshops across the country on the topic of the healing ministry to audiences that have included medical and mental health professionals, clergy, members of prayer groups and lay people who simply have an interest in the topic. And there have been questions in common from them.

They ask: "Who is called to minister, and how do they pray? How do we know who is called? How do we know what kind of healing is needed? Are there different kinds of prayers for different needs? How do we know when healing takes place? What do we do if there is no healing?"

In this chapter I will attempt to provide answers to these concerns, based on my experiences, my readings, and the experiences and knowledge of others who are ministers of healing.

Who is Called to Minister? How Do We Pray?

I believe each one of us is assigned certain people we are called to minister to for healing. Never, never refuse anyone who asks you for prayer. You do not know whether you have been designated to be a healing channel for that person.

If you do not pray over someone, I do not know how you can accomplish the will of the Father that you be made whole and holy and that you accomplish the works of Jesus. You should always perk up your ears when you hear Jesus saying "I solemnly assure you," and He said just that when He told us that those who have faith in Him will do the works He did and works far greater than even those. Why? Because He has the Father, and He will send the Holy Spirit.

Why are we so hesitant to continue His work when He wants to work through us? We hold back, and if we continue to hold back, we will never know how important it is for us to do His work. If we start doing it, we will find out what it is really all about. I have found that in the healing ministry, in groups where there is much praise for God, adoration, gratitude, honesty, the Spirit comes right into that group, stirs them into a fantastic powerhouse of healing prayer. These are spiritual people; we are all spiritual people belonging to the family of God.

But some of us are not aware that we are already filled with the Spirit; we are not aware of God's presence in our lives, and when we do become aware, that will make a difference. We will see the gifts that are there, we will uncover and discover them so they will come to light. That light is, precisely, Jesus walking with us, and we are within Him. We need to recognize within ourselves the power of the Holy Trinity, and reach out with faith, confidence and perseverance. The more we pray over others, the more we are blessed, so that we do not have to keep petitioning the Father for what we need. With that kind of charity shown to our brothers and sisters, all else is given to us in abundance besides.

To be healers we need to be lovers, taking God's affirmation and sharing it, being at all times a reservoir filled with His love, so it can spill over. We need to incorporate the attitudes of Jesus, see how He prayed to the Father. Just so, you can lay your hands on the sick, and they will recover. We need to be humble with faith, honest with hope, simple with love. Oh, Lord, teach us to pray. If you have these dispositions, you will find that the Lord, little by little, will use you as a healing channel.

Prayer is always a work of love. We are, however, so distracted by everyday routine that we forget God, forget we are witnesses of His power in our everyday lives, and no one speaks His words of assurance. "If you ask anything in my name, the Lord says, "I will do it." We only hear among us talk of solutions that are incapable of transforming life from within and from without. When we try to rely solely on our intellect, we forget that we can do nothing without Him.

I think sometimes we are just afraid to reach out and pray over someone, afraid that it will not "work," afraid that we will be ill-regarded, afraid, in fact, that we might fail. We must be bold, we must reach out in confidence. We get stuck believing that power was given only to the Apostles. He has given us power and the whole strength of the enemy. That is a lot of power, that is a lot of authority. Do not rejoice that the spirit submits to you, rather rejoice that your names are written in heaven and you share His power.

And building confidence in yourself as a conduit of healing is like building confidence in any role. You start with small things, enjoy small successes, before you attempt the bigger cases. Sometimes people get gung-ho after reading a few books on healing, and they figure they will wait for the biggie and attack that one — you know, wait for the person in the wheelchair. And then we try that, and nothing happens, and we say, well maybe that was meant for someone else.

The way to begin is with little things, little headaches, little bodies, little children. Children have no malice, they are so open, and they have no barriers to healing: so start with children. You know how it is with little ones. They have an injury. You kiss it. They forget about it because you were firm, and you poured love into them.

Young children especially get many ear infections. So pray for that. Address the infection itself. Say, **"You, evil infection we do not want you here, so in the name of Jesus Christ, you get out**

of here." Address pain the same way. Address it in the name of Jesus always, and tell it to go away. That is what does it.

Lay your hands on the sick, and do not hesitate. The Lord never said He would form a committee and think about it when someone needed healing. As novices we will have doubts, confusions, will be reluctant, will fail to dare. So begin where you are most familiar, begin in the family. Where you can learn most is within your own family. It is there that you are known best. It is there that you learn about forgiveness, concern, affirmation, support, generosity and love. The family is where you live, you study, you pray and stay.

You would not think twice about giving an aspirin to an ill child. Do not think twice about laying your hands on him or her and saying something like, "**This is my child, Lord. He is really a gift from the Father, and as His steward I am trying to do a really good job here. But he is suffering, and, Lord Jesus, You know what pain is. You went through all the pain anyone could endure, and You went through it for us. So by Your stripes, we are healed. I command this pain in my little child be lifted up in the stripes of Jesus to be healed. Thank you, Jesus. That is really neat for You to do that, to show us You love him.**"

And that is how we pray, simply, with love, with confidence and with honesty.

Honesty with God is important. I will tell you a story about that. I had a house which needed plumbing work, and my nephews did that work. But the plumbing inspector came and told me I had to rip out all the pipes because they were plastic and did not measure to code. I was also told that I probably got that order because I had failed to hire local plumbers for the job. After that happened, I said to the Lord, "Lord I am really angry with You. Here I am doing Your work seven days a week in that hospital, and You are supposed to take care of me, and this is what happens." Now that is a very honest prayer, right? It is honest because that is what I felt. He knows what you feel and wants you to come across with it, not trying to hide things in your heart. And He always has the last word.

Just after that, I received a phone call. Someone asked if I would be available to do some counseling. I said yes. That night the person who called pulled up in his truck. He was a plumber, a master plumber. I said to him, "You are my savior." I told him what happened, and he said he would take care of it. He spent the whole week with his helper installing the copper tubing I needed. I took the cost off his counseling bill, and he only charged me the cost of the materials. So I had to turn to the Lord, rather embarrassed. Not only did He help me, but He made sure it was a first-class job. That is what the Lord does when you are honest. Sometimes when you are angry, He gives back more than what you expect. So be honest, pray in your own words and from your own heart, and do not get involved in intellectual approaches.

You need to pray from where you are emotionally. If you are depressed, pray from your depression. If you are angry, how can you pray except to offer it to the Lord? Tell Him you are sad, tell Him you are angry. Pray without pretension.

And when we pray for healing for others, we do not need pretense, we do not need a show. Often it is appropriate to pray over a person when they do not know it. Nurses have a terrific opportunity to do this. They are always touching sick people. They can lay hands gently, pray over them silently.

Brother Armand Binet gives the following advice about praying over older children, teenagers, young adults who might not be receptive to laying on of hands and vocal prayer:

"When parents tell me that their children become restless and impatient when they try to pray over them, I tell them to wait until the child is at peace, or when the child is sleeping. Then you can pray over them. You do not have to touch them. Just pray that the Lord will fill them with Himself. And sometimes when you feel you cannot reach your children, that they will not listen to you, you have to be open and pray to the Lord that He send someone to your child who can communicate with him. Sometimes that person who can touch your child in that way will be someone you least expect to be able to do that."

Openness leads to unselfish prayer, and what St. Paul said about love can be applied to healing prayer. Effective prayer is "always patient, never boastful or conceited, rude or selfish; it is kind; it is never jealous; it does not take offense, and it is not resentful. It takes no pleasure in the sins of others, but delights in truth; it waits to excuse, it trusts, hopes and endures."

Whenever I have healing services, I pray before they begin. I always pray. I say the Rosary and ask our Blessed Mother that all over whom I pray will be touched by the compassionate healing power of Jesus Christ. I pray for compassion, and I pray for the gift of humility, because I have seen people in the healing ministry get so taken up with their popularity, and then they are not in the ministry any longer. They have taken part of the glory which belongs to God, because it is He who gives the power to do the work and bring wholeness and holiness to people.

Prayer always has two movements. The first is our approach to the throne of God, confident we are loved by Him, and that as we raise our voices as a community of faith, He will hear us and answer us. This petitioning movement is not complicated — you ask for what you have agreed as that community to ask for, and you do so with expectation that it will be granted, for you are so loved that Jesus wants to share with you His power.

For example, at a church in Santa Barbara, California a woman blind in one eye asked that we pray that her sight be restored. We did, petitioning that the Lord bring His kindly light, that it may shine in her eyes; that He cast away the darkness, and that His presence might be there so that she could see things clearly. When I asked her if there was any change, it was just like in the Gospel. She shouted out, "I can see, I can see." And we wonder whether the Lord is as powerful today as when He walked the streets of Jerusalem?

As we petition the Lord for graces and blessings, we need to prepare for the second movement of prayer, in which we express our gratitude that He heard us and answered us.

We need to be grateful. I did a healing service in a church in Carver, Massachusetts — the first time a healing service was held there. I asked whether any one wanted to be prayed over, and this man came up very distraught. I asked him what he wanted prayed for, and he just moved his mouth, but no sound came out. A woman was with him, and she said, "Two years ago he was in an accident, and he injured his spine and his vocal chords are paralyzed. He wants the Lord to restore his speech."

"Well, everybody, did you hear that?" I asked. Now in this small parish everyone knew everyone else. They all knew this man, and I asked them to pray for restoration of his speech. They did, and I prayed aloud. After a bit, without thinking, I handed the mike I had in my hand to this man and said, "Repeat after me, "Praise be to you, Oh Lord, Jesus Christ." And he did. Everyone in the church began to weep, because he had not uttered a sound in two years, and they knew they were witnessing a miracle — the compassionate healing power of Jesus Christ, right there in that little church.

And what did he speak after the prayer? He expressed his gratitude to Jesus Christ.

So the petition should be followed by gratitude. As we pray, too, we can bring to that petition authority that we already have, of which we may not be aware. For example, you receive great authority through the sacraments, and such power can be brought to bear on healing prayer. I know a couple — she is a psychiatrist, and he is a school principal — and when they work together, praying over people, they stand on the power of the sacrament of their matrimony, and people are healed.

The power, the authority given to us by Christ, our sharing in his dominion, certainly extends not only to the people of the world, but to nature, as well. I would like to quote here Brother Armand's discussion of this topic given at a seminar held at the La Salette Shrine in Attleboro, Mass:

"When we speak of natural events, we need to make a distinction between what is evil and what is demonic. Catastrophes such as mud slides are not good, they are evil, but they are not demonic, that is, they are not brought about by the work of Satan. What happens in catastrophes could be from nature, and to tell the difference you need in your prayer groups to pray for the gifts of the Spirit, one of which is discernment of evil spirits, the ability to tell what is of God and what is not, what is of God and what is of nature and what is of the flesh.

We can pray for things of nature because God has given us power over the world. I have done it myself, and I know it works. There is a powerful storm, we have power over that storm. He calmed the water and the winds, and He has given us power to do so. In many instances, Barbara Shlemon has stopped tornadoes. When she was camping in Florida, she heard that a tornado was headed for that camp ground, and she took command over it, and it split up as it hit the site, and no one was injured. I have taken command over storms, and it has stopped raining and thundering, and I have been able to go out and do the Lord's work."

(Editor's Note: Father Fredette's narrative resumes)

We also have authority over medications, and we should remember always to pray over any medication we are taking so that it will have no negative side effects. My cousin Dolly from South Carolina was in a wheelchair as the result of an accident, and she told me she got very drowsy from the medicine she was taking. I said I would bless it. I met her later, and she told me that the following evening she stayed up until 2 a.m. studying, took her medicine and was amazed that she stayed alert, and she remained alert after that despite the medication.

We should do that for ourselves and our children — pray over all medicines and procedures, such as x-ray, chemotherapy, whatever. It is a simple prayer I suggest. It is a blessing, and a blessing has two movements. The first part of the blessing is the casting out of anything that is not of the Lord. The second part is the invitation of the blessing upon the substance:

"Eternal Father, we ask You to bless this medicine (this procedure) and to neutralize all its side effects so that it will serve its intended purposes for the benefit of my health."

Such is the power of prayer. Taking their authority, too, from Christ, many physicians bring prayer to their work as part of their therapy. If you wish to see a psychiatrist or a psychologist, you should ask him or her whether he believes in prayer as part of therapy. If he says no, seek one who does, and there are many of those who are members of the Association of Christian Therapists. In that association we believe that prayer is indeed part of the treatment, that the therapist is really under the guidance of the Holy Spirit, and that it is really Jesus who is doing the therapy. We have insights we would not have on our own. We have discernment.

How Do We Know Who Is Called,
How Do We Know What Is Needed?

We are not all called in the same way to be healers; we are not all given the same gifts. But whatever gifts we are given, we should never fear we are going to lose them. It is a gift, and God is not an Indian giver. It is there all the time. If you do not use it, that is your problem. A well in the ground — if you do not use it, will develop a problem. It becomes filled with its own filth, and it does not fill with fresh, pure water. The more you use the well, the more the water will remain pure, and the same with our gifts from Him. The more we use them, the purer we become, the more attuned we become to the way He wants us to use them. We need to use them without fear.

How do you know what are your gifts? They will be revealed through discernment, and you can pray for discernment, which is itself a gift. It is an important gift for the healing ministry, the one needed most. For often people will tell you what it is they want you to pray for, a particular ailment, but the illness will only be an external symptom, with the source of the problem buried. The only way you will know that source is through discernment.

Pray first for openness to the word of God; perhaps something will strike you from Scripture — that opens the door to the gifts — and then pray for discernment. And pray as the Lord does. Go to your room. Close the door. Be in solitude. Then pray.

You need to ask the Lord about your charisms, the gifts given to use in the service of others. Pray, consult Scripture, ask the Lord to guide you, and then have your gift confirmed by a prayer group. It is important, to have the gift confirmed by someone outside you, with whom you pray who knows you. And of course, then you learn by doing. If you consistently pray over people for a certain kind of healing, and this healing occurs, then you know it is your gift.

For example, Francis MacNutt has a powerful, confirmed gift for the healing of bones. Many times cases of injured bones are referred to him because of his gift.

In my counseling, in my healing ministry, I had so many people to tend to that I needed to know quickly and efficiently what their needs were. So I prayed for the gift of discernment; every day I prayed for it, and it took three months for the Lord to answer my request.

For three months I asked every day, "Lord, please, I need this gift. I am doing your work after all." And after three months I was in the San Francisco area of California showing a film called "The Healing Power of Prayer" that was made at St. Vincent's Medical Center. After showing the film, I would ask if people wanted to be prayed over. One group led me to a man sitting in a chair, and I prayed out loud over him, and it turns out he was the pastor of the local parish. I did not know that. But what I had prayed for really reached him, because he was convinced that his parishioners had talked to me about him. He did not feel there was any other way I could have known what to pray for. And the people said, "Father Al, you have the gift of discernment." To show you how the Spirit works — that is how I got confirmation of the gift. And then I went to the next person, and I decided to pray silently, in my heart and spirit because I felt a prayer of deliverance was needed. This person was a tall man, sitting on the chair, waiting to be prayed over. So I bent my knee, put my hand on his back and prayed silently a prayer of deliverance. My hand got very warm, extraordinarily so. When we finished, he got up and asked who had a hand on his back because he said it felt like a hotplate there. Where I had put my hand was the site of cancer. How did I know this? I have discernment, and never, never will this gift fail.

Another time I was at a healing service at our shrine in Attleboro, and a man asked me to pray over him. I forgot what he asked me to pray for, but I prayed for it, and as he was leaving, I said, "Wait a minute, anything wrong with your ears.?" He said, "I cannot hear out of my right ear." I asked him whether he wanted me to pray for that, and he agreed. So I asked the Lord that it be opened. I then asked him if there was any change. He said, "I can hear the music," referring to the singing that was going on during the service.

Then I approached a different man, who was also being prayed over for something other than a heart condition. And I asked him, "Do you have trouble with your heart, and do you want us to pray for that.?" And he said, "Why, yes, I have an appointment with a heart specialist on Tuesday." And we prayed for that. So the Spirit helps us so that the prayers we use for one another may be effective and touch the area which needs completion, wholeness. That is discernment.

Interestingly, discernment does not always necessarily lead us to prayer as the only mode of healing. I did a healing of ancestry Mass in the Philippines, and one little boy in the family had a blocked ear. When I met the family a few days later I told them my discernment was showing me that the youngster needed surgery. The parents replied that the doctors insisted the same, but they, his mother and father, kept saying, "No, no, we will use prayers instead." But I said to them again, "My discernment is for surgery; go to the doctor and have the surgery, and your child will be healed."

This is an illustration of the gift of discernment, given by God to be used for the benefit of mankind.

So the Lord gives us these gifts so we can help others, and He guides us, and He speaks to us in different ways. I never thought I had the gift of physical healing, but God started to use me. And over a period of a few months, when I prayed for physical healing, people were healed. It built up my confidence. How do we know if we are discerning? How do we know whom to pray for, and for how long to pray for them and so forth?

There are natural ways and supernatural ways. To some people, God speaks to their reason. To others, He speaks through their emotions. Experienced healers through Christ like Barbara Shlemon say that they have feelings, intuitions, and hunches that help them to know who needs prayers and for how long and when healings take place. Some people have visions.

As a professional counselor, when people told me about hearing voices and seeing visions, I used to wonder. But now that it has happened to me, I have to take a second look at what they told me. Sometimes people will hear words at healing services, and know that an arm is being healed, or a foot, or an elbow, or a specific disease. Dr. McAll has visions all the time.

The gift of discernment will let us know what kind of spirits we are dealing with, and will prevent us from being deceived. We need to pray for protection against error, pretense and pride. And the best way to do that is to claim upon ourselves in protection the Most Precious Blood of Jesus Christ. It is important to do that each night before we sleep. Also we need to pray to protect the unconscious, so that dreams will not be disturbed and you have protection while asleep. Claim His Most Precious Blood upon your awareness, your subconscious, your unconscious and your collective unconscious. And then, when you dream, evil will not enter.

Different Prayers for Different Needs?

Although I have said that simplicity and not studied technique should define your prayer, there have been occasions in the healing ministry when a certain kind of approach is appropriate. The Linn brothers shared with me a healing which occurred during a retreat they held at a convent. Each day they would talk about spiritual matters and each evening they would have a liturgy. After the liturgy, they would pray over the nuns.

On the first night they learned there were two nuns who were completely blind, and so they prayed over them. Nothing seemed to happen. Then the next night the same thing. Now the Linn brothers are people who ask themselves a lot of questions. Dennis asked his brother Matthew, "Matthew, do you know what it is to be blind? Matthew said, "No, it is hard to imagine what it is like to be blind twenty-four hours a day." Dennis said, "I do not know what it is like either, so maybe we have to ask the nuns, the two blind nuns to pray over each other to gain sight."

They told the nuns, "Maybe you better pray over each other because you know what blindness is." So the nuns did just that, each asking the Lord to make her sister sighted. And every night those two nuns would pray for each other.

When they had the liturgy on the final evening, a Saturday, both nuns did the readings.

What do we learn from this? We learn that the ones most called to pray over one another at certain times are those who have experienced what the other person is experiencing. Sometimes at healing services I will ask if there is someone who has been healed of the same affliction who would be willing to pray over that person. If you had chronic arthritis and had been healed of it, you would be the one most likely to have compassion for another so burdened. If we have not had the disease we certainly can pray, but it is difficult to have the same degree of compassion as a like -sufferer. The prayer can be more effective coming from someone with a similar experience in life.

Those two nuns gained their sight because of the insight the Linn brothers had.

And there was another approach to prayer that I stumbled upon out of necessity. I was at a parish in Tucson, Arizona, and we had a Mass first, then the healing service, a combination which sometimes can be very long. We had five teams praying, and then a lady came to tell us that in ten minutes the pastor was going to turn off the lights. What can you say when the pastor is in charge?

A woman mentioned she was depressed. So I said, "Everyone here who is depressed — there must have been twenty people come forward — join hands in a circle." I told them we were going to pray about that depression, and not one of them could leave without smiling. I always visualize depression as a dark cloud oppressing the person, who cannot penetrate the darkness, and whose feelings are held inside, locked, and he cannot see the sunshine or the sunshine side of the cross. All he sees is suffering, and the pall of darkness holds all those negative emotions in, unexpressed anger, and so forth, and we need to pray that out. So I said a brief prayer to cast off the depression, and at the end everyone was smiling. Everyone was healed.

Then some people indicated they had heart disease. So I said, we do not have time to pray over you individually, so come form a circle. And so forth and so on with different ailments. And people came in groups, and they were healed.

So sometimes when crowds are great and time is short, such an approach works. Sometimes, when I am exhausted at healing services of great length where there are so many people in need, sometimes I just ask the Blessed Mother to take up my poor broken prayer and perfect it to make it effective.

How Do We Know When Healing Takes Place?

We have mentioned feelings of warmth and tears on the part of the person being prayed over as signs that healing has occurred.

Many people tell me they experience a feeling of tremendous heat in the affected area. With tears it is likely to be an emotional or psychological healing, a cleansing, and you know by that external symbol that something is going on inside. We have made reference to people in the healing ministry who receive signs of healing through discernment, through intuition, through specific words of bodily parts that have been healed. Also, sometimes we will witness new movement where there had been constriction or paralysis, and that attests to the healing.

At a healing service in San Francisco I came in through the back door, I saw a woman in a wheelchair, and I asked her what was wrong. She said she had multiple sclerosis. She told me she had been in the wheelchair for four years. I asked if she had a family. She said she had lost four children, and four survived. I said, "You ought to be home with your children, so make sure when we are praying over people, you are prayed over."

At the end, she was the last one. They wheeled her up. I asked the group to pray with me for our sister in affliction, and they did. We were having refreshments and in the corner of my eye, I saw her in the room. When I took a second look, she was getting out of the wheelchair. She began taking hesitant steps toward me. She walked in front of me and said, "Look, Father Al, I can walk." Four years in a wheelchair, but her movement was proof of her healing. I told her to keep returning to the prayer group and ask to be prayed over for continued strength. Here, she had gotten out of the wheelchair after four years. It was amazing.

Sometimes, especially in the case of broken bones, those praying over a person will actually feel through their hands the bones moving, knitting, healing. I recall praying over a woman who had arthritis in her hand, and I remember hearing the bones cracking as I was praying, and she was healed.

Following is the story of Todd Houghton, a 21-year-old physical therapy major at Northeastern University, Boston, Massachusetts. He relates what happened to him when at the age of 16 he was prayed over by Father Al. Todd was a member of the youth group at Our Lady of La Salette Shrine in Attleboro, Massachusetts at the time of his skiing accident. He presents his version, and Fr. Al tells what happened from his perspective:

Todd's Story: *"On January 31, 1987, I broke my leg while skiing in New Hampshire. I was first treated at a hospital there. But the doctors told me there was so much swelling the bone could not be set properly, so I came back home to Massachusetts. I was told by my doctors there the bone would not be set for several weeks because of that swelling. I was in a full hip cast. I was in a lot of pain. There was a jagged fracture like a bolt of lightening, and I was told it would not set perfectly. Some x-rays were taken, and what I did not know at the time was that the doctors were pretty sure a rod would have to be put in my leg.*

I clearly remember that I was home sitting on the couch, in awful pain, and Fr. Al came and prayed over me. My leg felt weird, very warm, and when he took his hands off the area, the pain was gone. He later told me he could feel the bones moving as he prayed.

After that, no more pain, and I had been on painkillers every four to six hours. The pain had been constant. I would wake up in the night screaming with the pain. Well, I returned to the doctor, and he said he wanted to take one last x-ray. I learned that he wanted the x-ray before he made the final decision on the rod because surgery was such a serious step with potential complications. Well, he came back with the x-ray and put it up on the screen and said, "Wait a minute, this is strange." And then he left to talk with another doctor. He came back to tell me that there had been more healing in the leg the past week than most people experience over the course of four months. Then he told me he had changed his mind about the rod. Because there was enough healing, the rod was not required.

I was in the cast for three months, and I was always a step ahead of what the doctors expected I could do. When they said I could lean on my leg, I was skipping on it. I did not need physical therapy. I did not need the rod, which might have interfered with my growth.

My mother told the doctor about Father Al. He said, somewhat skeptical, "Well, I don't know, but it worked didn't it?" And I have told people what happened and how I was healed.

Fr. Al's version: *"When I went to pray over Todd, I thought about the priest I had prayed over who had broken bones. So I said a command prayer, commanded the bones to move back into place and start mending. As I prayed I could feel the bones move. When I saw Todd a few weeks later, I asked him how he was doing. He said, 'Father Al, you will not believe this, it is healed, and I am moving my leg inside the cast.' When the cast was removed, there was perfect healing. The Lord does not do imperfect things.*

Later, when Todd told me he was influenced by his healing to pursue a career in a healing profession, physical therapy, I told him he was called to pray over his patients. He was relieved of pain, so he must serve as a channel to do that for others, praying silently. They do not need to know he is praying, and all he needs to say is: 'I command you, pain, in the name of Jesus Christ, leave this person.'"

Following is an anecdote offered by Patricia A. Kelly in illustration of internal physical movement as a sign of healing. The incident also, perhaps, provides another example of how sometimes the person most called to pray over another is the person who has experienced the same affliction:

"I was a member of a prayer team at a healing service conducted by Fr. Al in 1992 at a church in Seekonk, Mass. A woman came up to us and asked that she be prayed over for the healing of migraine headaches. Now I had suffered terribly from migraine headaches for many years, and I felt great compassion for this woman who was about the same age I was when I had these very painful headaches sometimes daily. It was almost as if I reexperi-

enced the episodes in flashback, and I could envision like in little film clips myself lying in darkened rooms — because when you have one of these headaches you cannot tolerate light; even the most muted light is magnified and is oppressive. I also had images of the depression and isolation I would feel when I had those headaches, and memory of the terrible pain which is very localized and has a quality very difficult to explain to people who have had only "ordinary" headaches.

Well, I laid my hand on her head, and as we prayed I felt the most unusual sensations. Migraine, of course, affects the blood vessels because it is a vascular headache, and as we prayed I could feel pulsating and movement beneath this woman's scalp. It was almost as if something was being surgically rearranged inside her skull. And the woman — she had initially sat so rigidly in the chair — completely relaxed, went almost limp, and under my hand it seemed that blood began coursing through her body from the head area. It was extraordinary."

What Do We Do If There is No Healing?

If the prayer is correct in what it is addressing, and nothing happens, or something only partially happens, then we must persevere in prayer. That is important. Sometimes what is needed is what is called "soaking prayer." The person may need to be prayed over repeatedly, and this is often true of afflictions which are deep-rooted, which have been chronic. Remember the story of the blind nuns who had to pray over one another on multiple occasions.

For example, when I was in the Philippines two years ago, a young man came down from the province to Manila. He had a growth on the side of his nose and inside the roof of his mouth. He underwent surgery, and he had not been able to eat normally for several months, being dependent upon a feeding tube. His mother asked us if we would pray over him. He could not open his mouth, could not speak. He was in pain. So we prayed over him, and he opened his mouth.

But his healing was not complete. I was there for a week, and his mother said he would be back. He returned, and I prayed over him again. He opened his mouth wider. Then again he came back, and I prayed, and he was able to begin eating with a spoon. Again, he returned, and there was more healing. So I told his family he needed soaking prayer. Sometimes healing is instantaneous, and sometimes it takes more time. The illness or infirmity seems to be frozen.

Other times when there is no healing, it is because there is a block. Discernment will tell you this and then you can pray out that block. When I was in the Philippines praying with a charismatic prayer group, a mother came with her little boy, who was about ten years old. I asked her what she wanted us to pray for, and she told me that the child had not been able to move his right arm since birth — that is a hurt of long duration. The arm was just hanging limply at his side.

When I finished praying I asked him to squeeze my hand. He reached out, took my hand and did just that. And then I asked the mother to take his hand. And the boy reached over and took her hand. She started crying because she knew that he had never done this in his life. Her tears were silent. This was a miracle.

All the doctors who had tended this boy had said there just was no way they could do anything. But I sensed the block, and it came to me that the bondage had to do with the child's ancestors. This was the very first time I had discerned that the block was in the ancestry. In the next chapter I will discuss this extremely important concept of healing of ancestry. Following is the prayer I said over this child, praying out the ancestral blockage to his healing:

Eternal Father, I ask the perfect humanity of Jesus Christ, Your Son, Our Lord, to touch every ancestor of this little boy. I lift up in the name of Jesus Christ, all the ancestors of this child who have never been baptized. I lift them up in the baptism of

desire. I assign them the names of the relatives and family members who lived at that time. And I now ask the holy angels to lead them into Paradise where they belong in the family of God with all the saints and angels. And I ask all of them now to be intercessors for this little boy right at this moment, that he may be released from the bondage that comes from the ancestry and that he may be bonded to Jesus Christ, Our Lord, through whom we are healed. I further ask Our Blessed Mother to take up this imperfect prayer, to perfect it, and offer it up to You, Eternal Father, in the name of Jesus Christ, Your son, Our Lord. We express our gratitude to You for healing this little boy because we know Jesus that you love children, take them up on Your knee and You bless them, and they are brought back to the fullness of life. We give You glory, Father, Son, Holy Spirit. AMEN

Chapter 6

HEALING OF ANCESTRY: RESTORING PEACE TO THE FAMILY TREE

Eternal Father. I adore You and give You thanks for creating me to be just who I am, for creating my genes, my life conditions, my space in life and time. You created me to enjoy the fullness of life, Your life in me. I believe You desire to make my family whole and that You have already begun to heal us in all the ways that need healing. We ask now that You take away our built-in defenses, today, that You remove all barriers that prevent healing. By fully accepting Your love for me and family members, I look forward to the time when Your work will be completed, and I believe that I will be a channel of that healing for my entire life.

Jesus, I ask You for the grace I need to forgive all who have ever hurt me, and I ask to be a representative of my family in receiving grace for all those who have hurt any members of my family, individually or collectively. I ask forgiveness from all whom we have hurt. Heal us, Lord, of all experiences that have caused us to be self-rejecting and rejecting of one another. Heal me of the rejection, real or imagined, of others. Heal me of ridicule or incidents in my life or in the lives of family members that have made us feel unworthy or inferior. (Take time

here, in this prayer, to ask the Holy Spirit to bring such incidents to your mind.) We ask now that You surround us with
Your light and penetrate, Jesus, the very depths of our being
with that light. Let there remain no areas of darkness within
me or within my family members, but transform our whole
beings with the healing light of Your love. We ask that You open
us completely to receive Your love, Jesus. We thank You for
being our family healer and our personal healer, too. We make
this prayer through Christ Our Lord. AMEN

Why Are We Not Healed?
The Answer Can Be in Our Ancestry

The healing of our ancestry is so important. Often when we
want to be healed and are not, often when we want peace restored
to our hearts and it does not come, the reason for lack of wholeness
and holiness is in our family trees. Maybe it is because we have not
forgiven an ancestor or ancestors, have not raised them up for prayer,
and there is still bondage there.

With our unforgiveness we bind up people who we say have
hurt us, and they remain bound after they die. They need to be
released by those they supposedly hurt. We need to know this and
share this knowledge with other family members, because where
we get hurt the most is in our families, with those whom we love
the most and who love us the most. If within our family we cannot
get on our knees, raise our hands and say, "help," then all the seminars in the world, traveling long distances to all the conferences in
the world to discuss spiritual matters, will not help us grow.

We begin to learn how to grow within the family context,
because that is where we are the same, yet different. Each one of us
is an individual, yet we also have within us some of the traits of
every other member of that family. The genes come down to us,
and added to the inherited ones are our own inclinations and attitudes, which may also be in need of healing.

We need truly to generate within our own hearts the intention, wish, desire that the Lord embrace each one of our ancestors who is in need of this completion. I learned in my counseling that it is very difficult for the individual to be healed if the family is not healed. If we are not healed of unforgiveness and negative traits and attitudes and bondages, then what we are doing is inheriting them, practicing them and then passing them on to future generations. We are responsible to our progeny, and it is up to us whether we pass on good or evil, and that is quite a responsibility. We need to take it seriously.

But we also need to remember that we inherit good, as well as evil from our ancestors. Gifts and blessings from God to the good people who have gone before us come down to us, too. Most of the time when we speak of healing of ancestry, we tend to talk about the negatives. We hear little about the positives, about the holy people in our families.

We should not curse our ancestors for the evil done, but forgive them. So the first movement of blessing our families is to ask that all the negatives be moved out to prepare the way for the coming of the Holy Spirit. In that Spirit, the Lord, Jesus Christ, who has the power, the healing power, the compassionate love will touch us in a way that we are made whole and holy. We ask that He come and preside over our family as we pray, especially the Eucharist, because that is where the power resides. So the first thing we do is clear the way.

For the second blessing we need to ask the Lord to make us aware of all the good people who preceded us, so we can give Him gratitude for them. We need to be healed of our unawareness of the goodness that preceded us — healed of the unawareness in our hearts and in our lives. We should communicate to one another that goodness when we become aware of it. Gifts and talents came from God to our ancestors, and we need to share in those talents and the love and the generosity and the gentleness and all the loving things they did — the way they lived Christian lives in times that were maybe harder than our times to live such lives. We need to be grateful to God for having created our ancestors. Remember He has created every one of us and our ancestors in His image.

The love of God comes down to us as the love of God came down to our ancestors. Yes, somehow in the struggle of life they failed here and there, and they sinned. But we should not be casting any stones. We should not be angry or resentful that our ancestors brought some discomfort to our lives. We need to forgive our ancestors for the ways in which they were not God- like. The Old Testament addressed badness, the sins of the father and grandfather going down for three or four generations. But St. Paul also says that when it comes to blessings, they go to the thousandth generation.

When we talk about healing ancestry, we are talking about inviting the Lord to enter into this space — there is no time and space for the Lord — to enter into these particular situations with our ancestors where there is need of healing. When we ask for healing of ancestry, we ask the Lord to embrace all family members past and present, known to us and unknown to us.

In all our backgrounds we have ancestors who died in dungeons, relatives who died unrepentant, unforgiving and unforgiven. We have ancestors who were not baptized, ancestors who had miscarriages and children not baptized, and ancestors who had abortions. We have unborn children in our ancestry who need to be lifted up in baptism of desire, who need to be given a name so they can have a place in heaven. The effects of abortion, let us call it what is is — the effects of murder — go on and on to future generations. I have found even in places where murder has been committed that somehow the whole area is polluted, and we have to bless that place.

We ask the Lord to embrace them all in a loving and forgiving way, so they can experience God's love unhampered by what bound them when they walked the dusty streets of this earth. And the Lord will. He does this. It is amazing. The world of the spirit is really interesting. It is more real than the material world. Start believing that.

Those who precede us do communicate to us of their need for prayer. We do not quite understand their language or the ways in which they communicate. Maybe some member of the family will be sick. Perhaps it is headaches. And then we remember that the person's father had headaches like that, and his grandfather, and all such negatives as the illness need to be cast out.

There are many things that hold people in bondage, many of them coming from ancestry. There is never just one, but a combination of elements that become oppressive. Emotions and feelings often need to be healed. I asked a friend of mine to share with us a history of her family that illustrates this point:

Following is a summary of the presentation made by a woman who witnessed at a workshop held by Fr. Fredette in 1991 for prayer groups on Cape Cod, Massachusetts. To protect her privacy, she asked that she not be identified in this book:

"Father asked me to explain to you an experience I had eleven years ago dealing with anxiety and panic and paranoia and depression. It usually occurs most severely after a trauma in one's life, such as a death in the family or maybe the birth of a baby — when even a year after the birth it is described as postpartum depression. Sometimes it occurs in a difficult marriage when one spouse feels put down all the time by the partner and may not even be conscious of that.

I realized that when I experienced these moods that they are extremely common, and very common among women, who do not share the experience because they feel they are alone in the situation. I think stress is a factor, and that a chemical imbalance may even result, and that such experiences usually happen to more than one member of a family and can be traced back generations.

My experience began eleven years ago when I lost a three-day old baby boy. About four months after his death, I felt a sudden burst of fear. I would ride in the car with my husband and experience this tremendous surge of fear. My mind would race, and I would think, "Oh, my house is on fire or something happened to my children." I would have an adrenalin rush, and I would try in my mind to figure out what was occurring. The episodes would end, and then happen again a day or two later. I also began having panic attacks, and I would feel the adrenalin rush, and then experience constriction of my throat, like I was choking. I started going to emergency rooms to tell doctors I was choking. They would say I was fine. I began to think there was something seriously wrong with me.

I went from doctor to doctor, and the fact they could find nothing wrong just increased my fear. Then I thought I was going crazy. These doctors cannot find anything wrong, and my body is responding at ninety miles per hour, and I must be going crazy. I have to be going crazy if all these doctors cannot find anything wrong. My mind would race with bizarre thoughts. I could no longer watch the television news or read newspapers. Because they would begin to trigger a fear in me.

I would be afraid of someone's conversation, thinking that, oh my goodness, if they say something they are going to scare me to death. Things just got worse. Soon I reached a level where I could not sleep or eat. I became paranoid, suspecting people knew I was crazy just by looking at me. I began to withdraw from people, and that was unusual since I had been outgoing all my life. So that was a strange response.

I was afraid of everything, including the doctors and the medicine the doctors prescribed. I did not believe it was going to work, and I feared I was never going to get better.

Anxiety filled my entire life. I believed I could not do anything right. So I did not even try.

I could not believe the day I discovered how many people, especially women, have suffered these same symptoms to some level or degree. You truly believe that no one could ever have felt this way before, and you figure you cannot share it with anyone because they would lock you up. So you hide within yourself in hopes no one will discover it.

Suicide crosses your mind because time just begins to seem endless with no hope in sight. You begin to not even trust yourself around other people because you feel you might be out of control. I began to fear that I would even harm my children because I was not in control. Even though, ironically, in most of these cases, the person affected is in far more control that he or she realizes. I felt so alone, so wrapped up deep within myself, and worry, fear anxiety, paranoia ruled my life.

Eventually I could no longer feel any emotion. I was emotionally dead. Everything shut down, and I lived in a void twenty-four hours a day. What I found out was that other family members had experienced this to some degree. I was very surprised to learn this. I found out that three of my sisters had experienced it to some degree. One sister, when she heard us talking about it, finally shared that she had experienced this after the birth of one of her children, and she never told anyone because she feared someone would put her away. She said she never shared it and was eventually healed of it.

As I talked with different people about this, I learned there are generational roots to this condition, generational ties. One of the psychologists I spoke with believed that anxiety is taught. He gave me an example. Maybe your mother, thinking it was in your best interests, when you showed her you made the honor roll, might have said, "That is a great job, but maybe you could have done a little better here or there." That was offered in hopes you could achieve more, but in reality what it taught you was anxiety — you are never quite good enough, but you are almost there — and that is passed on from generation to generation.

I found myself aware that I would use this attitude with my own children, and I had to correct that. The generational roots have to be cut — whether the problem is chemical or taught — or whatever way it is passed on from generation to generation. The roots have to be cut. And this is why the Mass for healing of ancestry works tremendously for people, and is a way of healing these problems. I praise God I came out of it, and that the Lord led me to Him eleven years ago. Thank you. "

109

Josephine (Joy) Chamberlain of Newburyport, Massachusetts, was so deeply touched by the depth and variety of healings she experienced following Father Fredette's celebration of a healing of ancestry Mass for her family that she wrote him a letter of thanksgiving detailing her experiences. Following are excerpts from this letter:

"*The intergenerational healing Mass has changed my life with the Lord's healing of past hurts. He used you, Father Al, and your ministry to heal a lifetime of scars which prevented me from really being free to love. God showed me I was a cripple in bondage to the pain of control, a hurt which I have come to realize we pass down to those whom we wish to protect.*

The day following the Mass I had a vision of my mother and father and the negative attitudes they had passed down which permeated my life and my growth. My mother was very religious, but there was a contradiction, as she also was into superstitions, spirits, fortune-telling, and confusion surrounded her. I believe when my mother became pregnant with me, she was considering leaving my father. My mother for years told me that a woman doctor had given her a pill to get rid of me, that she bled and was in pain, but that my father went to the drugstore and found out what kind of pill it was. My mother spent the nine months in bed, and during my childhood blamed me for 'holding on' and ruining her health.

I grew up insecure, frightened, accepting then that I was a 'bad' child and I sometimes acted rebellious. I also believe my mother felt guilt for what she had tried to do and that she passed on this guilt to me.

I was an ill child from birth and had to be nurtured, and my mother was loving when I was sick, but angry in between, as well as extremely domineering and controlling. She wanted to be loving and happy, but she had so many hurts herself that it was difficult for her.,

Father Al, when I talked with you you indicated a deep understanding of the impact that being an unwanted child can have on a

110

person's life. I realize now that my hurt has prevented me from being truly loving, and I am afraid that my children also have suffered my hurts. I realize that there is no need for the guilt I carry from my mother's unhappiness, and now I can begin to heal.

And in this healing, I can release my mother, who has been dead for 12 years. After the healing of ancestry Mass, I attended a retreat, which included a Mass during which I experienced an inner sensation of heat. I could hear Jesus telling me, "I will heal you of all your hurts so you can learn to love." The next day I had a vision of my mother holding me as a child and playfully bouncing me at her side as I said to her, "Ma, it was okay to be angry at me, but why were you so angry?"

It also took the healing of ancestry Mass to heal me of a situation that was potentially very destructive. In an experience reminiscent of my mother's attraction to fortune-telling, I was drawn in and manipulated by a Buddhist woman who could see things in my life, past, present and future. Unfortunately, then I did not realize that the source of her knowledge was evil. She was Vietnamese, and until the age of 12, she had been taught by nuns and priests. Her family told her she had to become Buddhist, and she became an ardent Buddhist. However, she had enough Catholic background to be able to confuse me. She would tell me that she loved the Blessed Mother, but when, despite her attempts to dissuade me, I went to Medjugorje and brought her back a huge picture of Mother Mary, she told me that she felt Jesus was a "little god."

I pray now that I can help others to realize what I did not at the time —that I was becoming involved with something not of God, being taken over by it. Whenever I would permit my doubts to surface, I would then feel I was too inept to make such a judgment. I even began to see her as a spiritual advisor, and when she told me about my flaws in a destructive way, because of my conditioning as a child, I accepted negatives as good for spiritual growth.

It was through your loving wisdom, Father Al, that I was saved from this situation and was able to seek healing through the ancestral Mass. I was being brainwashed and tricked by the devil oper-

ating through this woman, and I threw myself on the mercy of God and the Blessed Mother's love, and they sent me to you. I had told a couple of priests about this situation, but they could not give me the advice which saved me. I trusted entirely in a person. Now I trust entirely in God. I pray that your ministry continues to help many wounded souls, and that God will continue to grace you so that the healing power of Jesus will continue to work through you to those in need."

Places Need Healing, Too

These stories are examples of the kind of healings that families typically need. There are often ancestral roots to disturbances that are reflected in dwellings and in land areas and at other sites. The family tree has to be examined, and a healing of ancestry Mass said before peace is restored.

For example, the owners of a restaurant on Cape Cod called me to do a healing of ancestry Mass and a blessing of the site. They told me that there was a curve of road by the property where the incidence of fatal accidents had been extremely high, and they invited me to bless it. ' I did that, asking the Lord to come in, the Holy Spirit, calling down the angels to be sentries of protection for those who traveled the road. And I blessed the curve, their home, the business, including the bakery that was in back. I did that at five p.m., the closing time. And it was interesting. While I was doing the blessings, they decided not to close. And when I finished, they said, "You will not believe this, but we have never done such a volume of business in such a brief time, during the time you were blessing this area."

The Story of Dr. Michael Vigorito

I got a call one day from a dentist who said hesitatingly, "Fr. Al, I hear you believe in spirits and things like that. Would you be willing to come to a house I just bought for my business because we are having problems there, and the man who lives upstairs alone also reports disturbances. Will you bless the place?" I agreed.

Following is the story of Dr. Michael Vigorito of North Attleboro, Massachusetts, as told to the editor:

In February, 1987, Dr. Vigorito moved into a new office building he had purchased, and from the time he did, he said, "Strange things began to happen. It seemed like bad luck persisted, that if anything could go wrong, it did. Records and supplies were misplaced, and at first I chalked it up to confusion."

He relates an incident which occurred the day he moved his staff to the new location. A woman whom he had employed for three years and had been "almost like a member of my family" walked off the job after an argument and never returned.

"She had been such a good worker, but the first day she came to look at the new office she said, 'I don't like this place, it gives me the creeps. It feels like a morgue.' She refused to help in fixing up the office, and the closer it came time to move, the more unglued she became."

As unsettling events continued to occur at the new offices, Dr. Vigorito began to worry "whether I was losing my mind." He and staff members "kidded about the presence of poltergeists" and "I was under a great deal of stress, even contemplating selling the practice."

One day Dr. Vigorito heard water running from a tap in a laboratory, and when he was assured that no member of his staff had turned on a faucet, he entered the room to see the sink at the brink of overflowing. Another time he laid a letter on a front office desk

113

and left to get a stamp. When he returned the letter was gone, only to reappear in the same location shortly thereafter.

Matters came to a head the week before Easter when the dentist and his staff heard footsteps coming either from upstairs or in the waiting room. The tenant upstairs had gone to work. When Dr. Vigorito spoke to this man of the footsteps he "turned white" and was relieved to hear this information. "I do not know what to say," the tenant replied, "except I thought I was going crazy because there has been such weird stuff going on in my apartment." He then told Dr. Vigorito that he had heard footsteps on the roof of the house and had seen drawers open that he knew he had closed. On one occasion he found a shirt in another room that he knew he had draped over a chair in his bedroom. "I thought I was losing my mind," he confided.

Dr. Vigorito's friend worked at Our Lady of La Salette Shrine in Attleboro, Mass. and directed him to Fr. Fredette, who said, "I think those are more than coincidences. I think you have something there."

Fr. Fredette blessed each room in the office building, and following the blessing, Dr. Vigorito said, "I felt such peace. I was floating. I felt just great. I had not slept well in a couple of months, and I felt a weight had been lifted from me."

The dentist then told Fr. Fredette that he was having difficulty with his dentistry, that he felt "burned out and frustrated." Fr. Fredette asked him, "Who are you angry at, who have you not forgiven, what hurts have you not forgiven? If you want peace, you have to forgive."

Dr. Vigorito then called the woman whom he felt had hurt him, and he said he was sorry. "The remarkable thing was," said Dr. Vigorito, "that she said just a few hours earlier she had driven by my place and wanted to stop in and see me. After this, I felt much better."

Approximately one year later, similar incidents began to recur at the same location, "but with nowhere near the same intensity."

Fr. Fredette returned and blessed the rooms once more, and Dr. Vigorito says there have been no disturbances since.

The property in question was 33 years old when Dr. Vigorito purchased it, having been constructed on a vacant lot. It was designed to house a dental practice for a father and son, but the father was forced to retire before that became a reality.

The property is in an area where "King Philip," the American Indian Metacomet, sachem of the Wompanoags, waged war against the colonists.

A priest had blessed the building when it was constructed in 1954, bringing to three the number of times the site was blessed. (Fr. Fredette says that multiple blessings may be needed for disturbed environments, for "You need to beware that once the house is swept, it be kept swept." Sometimes, he says, you need to repeat the Mass and repeat the prayers.)

Dr. Vigorito's friend told him that one evening he passed by the property (before it was blessed the second time) to see an old woman rocking back and forth in a chair in the upstairs apartment. An elderly woman had rented that space many years from the previous owner and left there to die in a nursing home. Dr. Vigorito's brother told him of a couple who had fled an apartment in an adjacent house on the same street after they awoke one night to "see a mysterious figure hovering over the crib of their infant."

Fr. Fredette, in addition to blessing the business property, also said a healing of ancestry Mass at Dr. Vigorito's home. Dr. Vigorito said at that Mass a relative who had been somewhat estranged from the family cried during the Mass and embraced everyone, and that following the Mass, "the family was closer, more open and more inclined to overlook the little things which before that might have pyramided into major incidents and aggravations."

At the time of the Mass, Dr. Vigorito's grandfather was in a rest home in a senile condition. He subsequently died. Dr. Vigorito says he "idolized" this man until he learned of actions attributed to him that "shocked and hurt me." Fr. Fredette asked Dr. Vigorito to consider how God loved this person, to focus on the attributes which invited love. After doing that, Dr. Vigorito says he had a dream about his dead grandfather: "We were walking together down a dirt road, and my grandfather ran to a pond and tried to drown himself, and I saved him. "But then he went back in, and I yanked him out again. And then he went back in, and I realized then that I had to let him go. And after that, I saw him walking down the road, smiling. "

The Fruit of the Holy Spirit is Peace

The word "peace" is often used by those who have participated in healing of ancestry Masses to describe what they have experienced during and in the aftermath of this celebration. Peace is restored to people and places and situations, and order replaces chaos. Peace came to Dr. Vigorito's offices, and peace came to him in his sleep and in his dream of the grandfather he was able to forgive.

Following is the story of Viola Lynch of Weston, Massachusetts, who tells of the peace, and of the healings, personal and familial, experienced after Fr. Fredette said a healing of ancestry Mass at her home for her family, and the family of her husband Joseph:

"In June of 1992, Fr. Al Fredette said a healing of ancestry Mass at our home. One week after that Mass, I experienced a healing of relationship with my father and sister during a trip we made together to our ancestral countries, Austria and Czechoslovakia. This marked the first time we had been together since my mother died three years previously, and our relationship had been injured by absolutely devastating circumstances.

This was such a breakthrough. We were able to see each other through new eyes. Flashbacks, memories had been put in their place and we were able to live in the present and look forward to the future. We were able to let go, the atmosphere was defused, and

116

there was peace, and such graces for us. I realized that God was a
God of order, not confusion. We experienced a deeper forgiveness
and healing of the past than ever before, and were healed of anxi-
ety and more able to surrender our wills and our lives to God.
Since that time, as I would become a prayer partner with God, I
would be at Mass, and suddenly I would recall someone or a situ-
ation that needed prayer, and I would lift them up.

I also arranged for Fr. Al to say a healing of ancestry Mass for
other families that I knew. I invited to that Mass a mother and her
four children whose family had serious genetic disabilities, includ-
ing manic-depressive illness and alcohol abuse. Now before that
Mass, I served everyone dinner, and the children were extremely
restless, hyperactive. But as soon as the Mass began, all four, rang-
ing in age from 8 to 14, fell asleep on the couch, and their mother
was able to anoint them with the blessed oil that Father Al gave
her. And there was another woman there who also has a tough
generational situation. But she left before Communion. Perhaps
she could not yet deal with what the Holy Spirit was showing her.

I think the healing of ancestry through the Mass is so very, very
important, and I pass on Fr. Fredette's materials on this every
chance I get and encourage people to seek intergenerational heal-
ing this way."

Bless This Home

I always first bless the home which is to be the location of the
healing of ancestry Mass. This blessing can also be given when a
family moves into a new home or done yearly as a rededication.
Generally the people gather in the living room while it is being
done. Sometimes a family member or family members like to accompany me as I bless each room. Often a child wishes to follow
me. This is the format:

CALL TO WORSHIP

Leader: Peace to this house.
All: And to all who live here.

Leader: Let us pray.
Almighty and everlasting God, grant to this home the grace of Your presence, that You may be known to be the inhabitant of this dwelling, and the defender of this household. Through Jesus Christ, Our Lord, who with You and the Holy Spirit lives and reigns for ever and ever.
All: Amen.

WORD SERVICE

One of the family members reads a passage from the family Bible: Genesis 18:1-8; Matthew 10:1, 5-16; Luke 10: 38-42; Romans 12:9-16

INTERCESSIONS

Reader: May the Lord bless us abundantly in his love.
All: Blessed be God.

Reader: May the Lord grant us the spirit of peace.
All: Blessed be God.

Reader: May the Lord grant us the spirit of joy.
All: Blessed be God.

Reader: May we welcome all visitors here as Christ.
All: Blessed be God

BLESSINGS FOR GOD'S PEOPLE

Holy Angels, I call upon you to be sentries of protection for this home, property and possessions. I claim the Most Precious Blood of Jesus Christ upon all who live in this house, and all who visit here that all may forever be protected from all harm, injury, accident, illness and the wiles of the devil, that peace and harmony might reside here with those who dwell in this home blessed in the name of the Lord, Amen.

The leader may sprinkle the house with holy water. An image of Christ or the holy family may be prominently placed.

Leader: Visit, O blessed Lord, this home with the gladness of Your presence. Bless all who live here with the gift of Your love; and grant that we may manifest Your love to each other and to all whose lives we touch. May we grow in grace and in the knowledge and love of You; guide, comfort, and strengthen us, and preserve us in peace, O Jesus Christ, now and forever.

All: Amen

Following are the prayers, delivered by the leader, for blessing all the rooms individually, with each prayer to be followed by "Amen" from the assembled family:

At the **Entrance**: Sovereign Lord, you are Alpha and Omega, the beginning and the end. Send Your servants out from this place on many errands, be their constant companion on the way, and welcome them upon their return, so that coming and going they may be sustained by Your presence. Through Christ our Lord.

In the **Living Room or Family Room**: Bless this living room that here we may find our bonds of friendship joyfully renewed and deepened after days of study and work, play and growth. May Your peace always stay in this room, making it a place where we can each grow into better friends with You and with one another. Through Christ our Lord.

In the **Kitchen**: O Lord our God, You supply every need of ours according to your great riches. Bless the hands that work in this place, and give us grateful hearts for daily bread. Through Christ our Lord.

In the **Dining Room** or Area: Blessed are you, O Lord, King of the Universe, for You give us food and drink to sustain our lives. Make us grateful for all Your mercies, and mindful of the needs of others. Through Jesus Christ our Lord.

In a **Bedroom**: O God of life and love, the true rest of Your people. Sanctify our hours of rest and refreshment, our sleeping and waking, and grant that strengthened by the indwelling of the Holy Spirit, we may rise to serve You all the days of our life. Through Jesus Christ our Lord.

In a **Child's Room**: Heavenly Father, Your Son our Savior took children in his arms and blessed them. Embrace the child whose room this is with Your unfailing love. Protect him/her from all danger and bring him/her in safety to each new day until he/she greets with joy the great day of Your kingdom. Through Jesus Christ our Lord.

In a **Guest Room**: Loving God, You have taught us to welcome one another as Christ welcomed us. Bless those who from time to time share the hospitality of this home. May Your protective care shield them, the love of Jesus preserve them from all evil, and the guidance of Your Holy Spirit keep them in the way that leads to eternal life. Through Jesus Christ our Lord.

In a **Bathroom**: Father, You gave us bodies that we might be the living body of Christ on earth. Grant a blessing which fills this room, so that out of love for You we may always care for our bodies as the living temples of Your Holy Spirit. Through Christ Our Lord.

In a **Recreation Area or Backyard**: Father, You richly shared Your precious gift of life with us. Bless this place of rest and leisure time, that in our play and recreation, we may find refreshment and fulfillment for our busy lives. Through Christ our Lord.

In a **Workroom or Workshop**: O God, Your blessed Son worked with his hands in the carpenter shop in Nazareth. Be present, we pray, with those who work in this place, that laboring as workers together with You, they may share the joy of Your creation. Through Christ Our Lord.

Exchange an embrace or gesture of love. All may join in a song of praise.

The Story of Nathaniel

The story of Nathaniel provides an example of multiple healings, a story of deliverance and the need to restore peace to a disturbed child, a disturbed family and a disturbed property. One day, as I was engaged in counseling at the shrine of Our Lady of La Salette, I got a telephone call from a woman. She said, "Father, you are our last hope." Now whenever those words are spoken, I will guarantee you that means a cry for deliverance.

She said she had a little boy named Nathaniel and that he was five years old and there was something terribly disturbed about him. He did not sleep at night. He stalked around the house. He rummaged through drawers and had grabbed a knife and threatened to kill his little sister. Sometimes when he walked down the street, his facial features changed into an ugly grimace. Often he would try to dart in front of cars as if he were trying to kill himself.

His doctor said there was nothing wrong with him physically. A psychologist said he could not determine the problem. A psychiatrist agreed that the child was disturbed, but, again, could not present a diagnosis. The psychiatrist recommended drug therapy.

So I told her to bring the child to me. She asked if she could also bring a priest who was a friend of hers, whose name was also Nathaniel, and a neighbor. They arrived at about 11 a.m., and I was scheduled to say Mass at noon. He was a nice little boy, and I said to him, "Nathaniel, here is what we are going to do. I am going to sit in front of you, hold your hands, look in your eyes and pray silently. I did not tell him I was going to say a deliverance prayer. But when I started to pray, his eyeballs rolled, and I could only see the whites of his eyes.

I stopped, knowing there was interference, evil things going on. Then I tried to pray once more, and he started howling like a wolf. There was chaos and confusion in the whole room. I stopped praying then, and I told the mother there was nothing more to be done at that moment, but that she should consider having a healing of ancestry Mass said. I told her there was some kind of ancestral bondage here. She took a set of instructions for preparing the family tree, and we set a date to bless the house and say the Mass.

I went to say the noon Mass at the shrine, and during the prayers of petition I told the people that I share my ministry with them because they are part of the community of faith which supports it. I said that I saw a little boy that morning whose mother was distraught and that the little boy was "restless." "How would you mothers feel if your child was restless?" I asked. Wouldn't you want prayers for him?" They agreed, of course, and they all then prayed for Nathaniel.

At Communion time a woman came up with a little boy, and I asked her whether she would come to the sacristry after Mass, and I asked Father Nathaniel — who had stayed — to come there also. When she came with her son I asked her if he could sit in proxy for Nathaniel so we could pray over Nathaniel because proxy prayers never fail. By the way, this boy's name was Nathaniel also. So I said a quiet prayer of deliverance over the child who was sitting in proxy. I prayed that all fear, disturbances, doubts be cast out of him, that he belonged to Jesus and the devil had no business disturbing him. They left, and in a few days I got a call from his mother.

This is how Nathaniel's mother describes this telephone call she made to Fr. Fredette:

"I told Father that by the time we had completed the drive home which took about an hour, my son was a completely changed person. His features appeared calm, and he was so polite. In fact he had slept all the way home. When he got home he took a candle out of his birthday cake, went into my bedroom and put his picture in the frame which held a picture of the Sacred Heart of Jesus and put the candle in front of that."

When Nathaniel's mother came back to the shrine to bring the family tree she had prepared, I asked her how things were going. She said that there was an incident that had the family in turmoil. She explained that her husband normally works at night, but this night he stayed home. He woke her up and told her he heard footsteps in the attic. She said it was mice, but he was sure it was human footsteps. He got up terrified and left the house in the middle of the night. The next day she put a trap in the attic and set it with bait. When she checked the following morning the bait was gone, the trap was not sprung. Then a stray cat came to the property, and she put him in the attic. That evening they heard noises from a terrible fight, and when they climbed to the area after daybreak, they saw blood in the attic, which was boarded up. The bait was gone, and there was no sign of the cat.

Their final strategy was to put flour in about a six-foot circle around the baited trap. But again, when they checked, the bait was gone, the trap was not sprung, and there was not a sign of a footprint.

I said it was time to say a healing Mass on the property. Nathaniel's mother also said that the family had been beset by problems since they moved into the house, which was built in colonial times. She indicated that in the 1800's a slaughterhouse had been operated on the grounds by the founder of a major meat-packing company.

She said the children had been plagued with illnesses and accidents; that doors to cabinets and rooms opened and shut on their own; that a swimming pool they attempted to build kept collapsing; that they had repeated malfunctions of their heating systems which blanketed the interior of the house with soot; that the horn on their jeep triggered at night in a pattern of beeps which appeared to be a code.

When I arrived on the property and started walking to the house, I said to myself, "Wait a minute, I sense there has been murder here," and where there has been murder we need prayers for the repose of souls. Nathaniel greeted me, and I asked him to follow me around the land while we blessed it with holy water. Nathaniel's mother then told me she had checked records at the town hall and learned that her land was the site of an Indian massacre. So all those Indians were murdered there, and all their souls were crying out for prayer.

I went into the house and saw the trap that had been set for mice, but I knew it was not mice that were infesting the house. I asked Jesus during the Mass I said to bless all the members of that family so that His perfect humanity would enter the situation where needed. We also lifted up in the name of Jesus Christ all the souls of the babies in the families who had not been baptized, the souls of miscarried, aborted children. We lifted them up in a baptism of desire and gave them names that were common in this family. And we asked that the angels lead these children to Paradise so they could take their rightful place with God and become intercessors themselves for this family that was so afflicted.

Two years later, Nathaniel's mother called me to tell me that he was going to make his First Communion that coming Sunday and insisted that I give it to him, that he would not take it from anyone else. So I was saying Mass at Otis Air Force Base that day, and she came with Nathaniel, who had been a very good student his first years of school and who had suffered no more disturbances. "Well," I said, "I will give him Communion." After I did that she asked Nathaniel to tell me what he wanted to be when he grew up. He said, "Fr. Al, I want to be just like you."

What a compliment I thought. This boy had been freed from all kinds of evil, spiritual, emotional, physical difficulties, and he radiated joy and peace, the gifts of the Holy Spirit, and he was growing up in wisdom and grace, just like Jesus. It is really something to see how the Lord listens to our prayers and hears us when we lift up our ancestors in prayer.

At the conclusion of a healing of ancestry Mass I always ask if there is anyone in the family who wishes to be prayed over for any kind of affliction, and healing does occur for the present generation.

Following is the story of Renee, Dennis and Bryan Gall of Buckman, Minnesota, whose family experienced individual healings after Fr. Fredette said a Mass of intergenerational healing at their home. Mrs. Gall relates:

"On October 14, 1990, our son Bryan was critically injured in a collision of a three-wheeler and a pick-up truck. An artery was severed, and his left arm had to be removed. We were told he was dying, but I did not want to believe that. We were told his chances for living were a drop in the ocean, next to zero, and we went away from the hospital without hope. My sister urged us to still have hope, and we went to Mass and prayed. The community was praying for him too. And praise God, things did change, and Bryan

came out of the coma and left the hospital for a nursing home specializing in long-term care for victims of severe head injuries.

Fr. Al said a healing of ancestry Mass at our home. We have big families and many came to the Mass, packing into the downstairs room.

On a day after the Mass Bryan was home and I wanted him to nap, so I propped myself up with pillows beside him to ask him some questions, but I fell asleep. While I was sleeping he came downstairs, and my daughter asked Bryan where I was. Bryan said, "She is upstairs asleep in my room." While that may not sound significant, it was. By saying that, Bryan showed that his short-term memory had returned for the first time since the accident. He still has good days and bad days, and Father says he needs soaking prayer. But he has started walking with a cane now.

There were several healings in our family after that Mass. My brother-in-law had experienced such pain in his hip and leg that during the sign of peace he would hardly stand, and was taking ten to twenty pills per day. He has no need of medication now. Another brother was prayed over for lower back pain, and it disappeared. My brother had pain in his neck and shoulder, which left him after the Mass. We also prayed by proxy for a baby in the family who could not come, but who suffered a terrible rash on his face since birth, with the theory being he was allergic to his own tears. After the Mass, his faced cleared."

Following is Patricia A, Kelly's story, recounting healings experienced after Fr. Fredette said a healing of ancestry Mass in her home:

"Fr. Al was juggling two dates for the saying of this Mass in our home —October 4, 1991, and October 5, 1991. The Mass was celebrated on October 5, but both these dates appeared as significant ones after I and my husband researched our family trees. I discovered that October 4, 1941 was the day my parents (both deceased) were wed —not the date they had told their children was

their anniversary. In fact, throughout their married life, they stead-
fastly refused to celebrate their wedding anniversary, and chose
instead to observe the day they first met. I learned that the
October 4th marriage was an elopement, and the fact of this wed-
ding day was not shared with their families for many months, and
never shared with their children. I felt a great relief receiving this
information, which explained tensions and anxieties which per-
sisted, especially in my mother's life. The releasing of this "se-
cret," which I came across in reviewing the records of my father's
conversion to Catholicism, brought healing knowledge to me.

Following the Mass, my husband's aunt, who attended, wanted
to discuss an ancestor on the family tree whom she felt had been an
extremely disruptive influence. My husband told her that in his re-
search he had discovered a "secret" about this man's lineage, and
he told her what he had learned. She expressed enormous relief at
hearing these facts. Later, when Fr. Al had left, we looked closely
at the family tree my husband had compiled to discover that Octo-
ber 5, the day of the Mass, was the birthday of this ancestor.

That evening, after the Mass and the blessing of our home, I
had a compelling dream, which moves me to tears each time I re-
call it. In the dream a young man who looked enough like my
younger brother to be his twin, was dressed in what appeared to be
a hospital gown. He was standing in stark surroundings, concrete
walls, concrete floor. His hair was very long, curling over his shoul-
ders. He was shuffling across the floor. Suddenly, it appeared that
he was struck by some kind of vision or realization. His head, which
had been drooped near his chest, went suddenly back, and his fea-
tures mirrored sudden knowledge and joy. He outstretched his arms
and began to walk towards something. It was as if he had gone
from darkness, abandonment, hopelessness, imprisonment, to re-
lease, freedom and light. After that dream, I awoke to hear very
purposeful footsteps which began inside the front door, continued
up the front stairs and ended at the foot of my bed. I was not fright-
ened by the presence I momentarily felt in the room. It was as if
someone was hovering there in a kind of thanksgiving.

127

It was also shortly after the celebration if this Mass that I was moved to take our young son, whom we adopted from Ecuador, to see the Missionary Image of Our Lady of Guadalupe. Our son's biological heritage is Hispanic and Mayan Indian, and he has suffered with the knowledge that he will probably never know his biological mother. He was mesmerized by the picture of Our Lady, touched his Rosary to it and then sat on my lap by the Image silently for a long time. Then he said, "Mama, I look just like her." And, of course, this was true. The issues of adoptive/biological mother faded in this healing that came from bringing him to the Blessed Mother, to the specific Image of her that was so special, so individualized for the culture to which she appeared. And it was not until I visited the Image with him that I realized that the December day we arrived in Ecuador and attended Mass there to pray for our son (who was then in an orphanage) was, in fact, the feast day of Our Lady of Guadalupe.

Dear friends of mine, Helen and Dave Logan of Plymouth, Massachusetts told me of their "adoption story" which also reached a healing conclusion after Father Al said a healing of ancestry Mass in their home. Helen and Dave had a daughter when they were sixteen years old and unmarried, and they placed her for adoption through Catholic Charities. They later married and had two other daughters and a son. One day after the Mass they received a letter —which reached them despite the fact it carried a wrong address —indicating that their first-born daughter had searched for her birth parents and wished to meet them. They were overcome with joy, as they had prayed for her each day since her birth. They and daughter "Merri" are now part of each others lives, and the brothers and sisters have been reunited.

Preparing for the Healing of Ancestry Mass

1. Make a Family Tree in writing. Put down the name of ancestors, as well as you can remember them. Indicate whether there was a problem with any of them, physical, emotional, psychological, or whether they died violent deaths. For example, "Aunt Sarah was manic-depressive," Uncle Joseph was alcoholic," "Grandfather Samuel died mysteriously." "Grandmother Emily had migraine headaches." Give the first name of the ancestor or relative and indicate the difficulty. Give the blood lines of father and mother/husband/wife relatives.

2. Pray to the Holy Spirit to enlighten you in these matters as you prepare the tree, and to bring to light the names of the relatives, ancestors who were holy people, saintly people.

3. Make sure you disclose all that you do know on this family tree, which should be burned or otherwise destroyed following the Mass. One time I said a healing of ancestry Mass at a family's home and was called back later and told that things only got worse at the home: nails were coming out of the wall, the car blew up, the husband lost his job. I asked the wife whether she deliberately eliminated anything from the family tree. Well, she said yes, and mentioned things she considered shameful — alcoholism, drug addiction, this person being jealous, another lustful, another with the spirit of retaliation. " What do you want?" I asked. You cannot fool God. On the condition that you are sincere, you do the best you can, then the Lord will come into the situation. But if you are going to be dishonest with Him, He will not work with you."

4.   When this is done, present the material to the priest who will be saying the Mass so he can review it and set a date for the celebration, which will also include the blessing of the home.

5.   Family members should be invited to attend the Mass. However, no one should be pressured to attend who objects. Also it is a good idea to prepare by listening to my tape cassettes on healing of ancestry.

Following Is the Healing of Ancestry Mass, in full text, with its special prayers, just as it is celebrated by Fr. Fredette in the homes of all who request it:

MASS OFFERING FOR HEALING THE FAMILY TREE

Lord, I offer this Eucharist for all of our ancestors and relatives living and dead, especially those who are not at rest, or who died an evil death, lacking the proper rites of the Church and Christian community. I commit them to You that You may grant them eternal rest, peace and happiness.

I ask forgiveness and reparation for our sins that have contributed to the prolongation of hurt in our family. I ask Your forgiveness for, and the grace that I may forgive those whose sins, known and unknown, have harmed our family from within or without, that reparation may take place.

I also include and commit to You in this intention any children lost through abortion, miscarriage, stillbirth, or given up for adoption, that they may be received by and fulfilled in You. We make our prayer that all members of our family tree, living and dead, may have Your mercy, forgiveness, conversion and healing and be received into eternal glory. In Jesus' name, we pray. AMEN

INTRODUCTORY RITE

Leader: Acts of prayer and penitence prepare us to meet Christ as He comes in Word and Sacrament. We gather as a worshiping, believing community to celebrate our unity with Him, with our family members, living and dead, and with one another in faith.

The Entrance Song should follow.
Suggested is "Here I am Lord," by Dan Schutte.

Priest: **Welcome to those present and to those whom we represent as family. Let us begin by invoking the power of Jesus' Cross to deliver the living and the dead from all evil.**

All: In the name of the Father and of the Son and of the Holy Spirit. Amen

Priest: **The grace and peace of God our Creator and the Lord Jesus Christ be with you.**

PENITENTIAL RITE

Priest: **As we prepare to celebrate the mystery of Christ's love, let us acknowledge our failures, and the failures of family members and ask the Lord for pardon and strength.**

All: Lord, You have commanded us to love our enemies, to do good to those who hate us, to forgive those who have cursed us, and to pray for those who persecute us.

Lord, I ask You to show us the ways in which I and my family members have hurt each other, especially those who are now deceased. Show us attitudes and behaviors I have criticized in those deceased that are also part of us who are still living.

(Pause for reflection).

I forgive all those in my family living and dead who have hurt us in any way. I forgive all those who are still unrepentant of what they have done. I give them permission now to forgive us, and I also forgive myself, Lord. Where I have placed blame on You, I ask forgiveness of You, Creator God.

Jesus, show us how You want to heal and love the deceased in my family during this Eucharist.

Leader: You raised the dead to life in the Spirit. Christ have mercy.

All: Christ have mercy.

Leader: You bring pardon and peace to sinners. Lord, have mercy.

All: Lord have mercy.

Leader: Fill us with your forgiveness, Lord.

All: Lord, have mercy.

Leader: May almighty God have mercy on us, forgive us our sins and bring us to everlasting life.

All: Amen.

Leader: Today's Mass is being offered for our family systems: for the healing of those negative patterns of behavior, addictions, sickness of mind and body, diseases, vulnerabilities, handicaps, and any other unhealthy conditions.

For the removal of any curses and external negative forces from any sources that affect our family members;

For the special gifts, talents, human powers and virtues to be reclaimed and owned by our family members;

So that we may come to know now and in future generations the perfection to which we have been called to become in the image and likeness of God.

OPENING PRAYER

Eternal Father, we entrust to You our brothers and sisters and all our ancestors who have preceded us, that they may live with You forever. By Your merciful love wash away whatever sins they may have committed in human weakness while they lived on earth.

We ask this through our Lord Jesus Christ, Your Son, who lives and reigns with You and the Holy Spirit, one God, forever and ever.

FIRST READING

A reading from the book of the prophet Isaiah
(Is 11:1-10)

He judges the poor with justice

A shoot shall sprout from the stump of Jesse
and from his roots a bud shall blossom.
The spirit of the Lord shall rest upon him:
a spirit of wisdom and understanding,
a spirit of counsel and strength,
a spirit of knowledge and fear of the Lord,
and his delight shall be the fear of the Lord.
Not by appearance shall he judge,
nor by hearsay shall he decide,
but he shall judge the poor with justice,
and decide aright for the land's afflicted.
He shall strike the ruthless with the rod of his mouth,
and with the breath of his lips he shall slay the wicked.
Justice shall be the band around his waist,
and faithfulness a belt upon his hips.
Then the wolf shall be a guest of the lamb,
and the leopard shall lie down with the kid;
the calf and the young lion shall browse together,
with a little child to guide them.
The cow and the bear shall be neighbors,
together their young shall rest;
the lion shall eat hay like the ox.
The baby shall play by the cobra's den,
and the child lay his hand on the adder's lair.
There shall be no harm or ruin on all my holy mountain;
for the earth shall be filled with knowledge of the Lord,
as waters covers the sea.

On that day, the root of Jesse,
   set up as a signal for the nations,
The Gentiles shall seek out
   for this dwelling shall be glorious.

This is the word of the Lord.

All: Thanks be to God.

RESPONSORIAL PSALM
(Is 38:10,11,12,16)

R.   You saved my life, O Lord; I shall not die.

Once I said, "In the noontime of life I must depart. To
the gates of the nether world I shall be consigned for
the rest of my years."

R.   You saved my life, O Lord; I shall not die.

I said, "I shall see the Lord no more in the land of the
living.
"No longer shall I behold my fellow men among those
who dwell in the world."

R.   You saved my life, O Lord, I shall not die.

My dwelling, like a shepherd's tent, is struck down and
borne away from me; You have folded up my life, like a
weaver who severs the last thread.

R.   You saved my life, O Lord; I shall not die.

Those live whom the Lord protects; Yours alone is…
the life of my spirit. You have given me health and life.

R.   You saved my life, O Lord; I shall not die.

SECOND READING

A Reading From the Letter of James
(Jas 5, 13-16)

The prayer of faith will save the infirm man.

If anyone among you is suffering hardship, he must pray. If a person is in good spirits, he shall sing a hymn of praise. Is there anyone sick among you? He should ask for the elders of the church. They in turn are to pray over him, anointing him with oil in the Name of the Lord. This prayer uttered in faith will reclaim the one who is ill, and the Lord will restore him to health. If he has committed any sins, forgiveness will be his. Hence, declare your sins to one another, that you may find healing.
This is the word of the Lord.

All: Thanks be to God!

ALLELUIA

Alleluia, Alleluia, Alleluia

Verse: He took our sickness away, and carried our diseases for us.
Repeat: Alleluia

Leader: The Lord be with you
All: And also with you.

GOSPEL

A Reading from the Holy Gospel According to Mark
(Mark 16, 14-20)

They will place their hands on the sick and they will recover.

Jesus appeared to the Eleven and said to them: "Go into the whole world and proclaim the good news to all creation. The man who believes in it and accepts baptism will be saved; the man who refuses to believe it will be condemned. Signs like these will accompany those who have professed their faith; they will use my name to expel demons; they will speak entirely new languages; they will be able to handle serpents; they will be able to drink deadly poison without harm, and the sick upon whom they lay their hands will recover." Then, after speaking to them, the Lord Jesus was taken up into heaven and took His seat at God's right hand. The Eleven went forth and preached everywhere. The Lord continued to work with them throughout and confirm the message through the signs which accompanied them.

This is the word of the Lord.

All: Praise be to you, Lord Jesus Christ.

GENERAL INTERCESSIONS

Priest

(or Leader): **As a priestly people we unite with one another to pray for today's needs in the Church and in the world.**

All: Lord hear our prayer.

Priest: For the healing of all the effects of the drug culture.
All: Lord hear our prayer.

Priest: That addictions to all things be healed, especially addictions to alcohol, power, security, pleasures of the world, that all may experience the freedom of God's love.
All: Lord hear our prayer.

Priest: For the conversion to God's love of those involved in satanic worship and other evil cults.
All: Lord hear our prayer.

Priest: For the healing of the earth.
All: Lord hear our prayer.

Priest: For family unity, love, and respect for one another.
All: Lord hear our prayer.

Priest: For the healing of violence and abuse of one human to another.
ALL: Lord hear our prayer.

Priest: For the aborted children, the miscarriages, the still-born and all who were never baptized in our families, that we may own and claim them all for the Kingdom of God.
All: Lord hear our prayer.

Priest: For those in authority in the Church and in the world, to use their positions with justice, mercy and wisdom.
All: Lord hear our prayer.

Priest: Add your own intentions.
All: Lord hear our prayer.

LITURGY OF THE EUCHARIST

Leader: We offer to God the gifts of the deceased members of our families and thank God for all the good that has come to us and others because of them. We ask for the vision to see the ways in which their lives have brought forth great mercy and forgiveness. Whether we are blind to our family's goodness or not, we now offer it with love and ask the Creator to bless that goodness and all the ways it has been shared with others.

Offertory:
We place our Family Tree and petitions on the altar.

Preparation of the Bread:

Priest: **Blessed are You, Lord, God of all creation. Through Your goodness we have this bread to offer which earth has given and human hands have made. It will become for us the bread of life.**

All: Blessed be God forever.

Preparation of the Wine:

Priest: **By the mystery of this water and wine, may we come to share in the divinity of Christ Who humbled Himself to share in our humanity.**

Blessed are You, Lord, God of all creation. Through Your goodness we have this wine to offer, fruit of the vine and work of human hands. It will become our spiritual drink.

All: Blessed be God forever.

Priest: **Lord God, we ask You to receive us and be pleased with the sacrifice we offer You with humble and contrite hearts.**

Lord, wash away our iniquity; cleanse us from our sins.

Invitation to prayer:

Priest: **Pray, sisters and brothers, that our sacrifice may be acceptable to God, Our Father in heaven.**

All: May the Lord accept the sacrifice at your hands, for the praise and glory of His name, for our good, and the good of all His Church.

PRAYER OVER THE GIFTS

LORD, be merciful to Your servants, all our family members who have died and for whom we offer You this sacrifice of peace. They were faithful to You in this life; reward them with life forever in Your presence.

We ask this through Christ our Lord.

All: Amen.

EUCHARISTIC PRAYER
FOR MASSES OF RECONCILIATION II

Priest: **The Lord be with you.**
All: And also with you.

Priest: **Lift up your hearts.**
All: We have lifted them up to the Lord.

Priest: **Let us give thanks to the Lord our God.**
All: It is right to give Him thanks and praise.

Priest: Father, all powerful and ever living God, we praise You and thank You through Jesus Christ Our Lord for Your presence and action in the world.

In the midst of conflict and division, we know it is You who turn our minds to thoughts of peace. Your Spirit changes our hearts: enemies begin to speak to one another, those who were estranged join hands in friendship, and nations seek the way of peace together.

Your Spirit is at work when understanding puts an end to strife, when hatred is quenched by mercy, and vengeance gives way to forgiveness.

For this we should never cease to thank and praise You. We join with all the choirs of heaven as they sing forever to Your glory:

All: Holy, holy, holy, Lord, God of power and might. Heaven and earth are full of Your glory. Hosanna in the highest. Blessed is He who comes in the name of the Lord. Hosanna in the highest.

Priest: God of power and might, we praise You through Your Son, Jesus Christ, Who comes in Your name. He is the Word that brings salvation. He is the hand You stretch out to sinners. He is the way that leads to Your peace.

God, our Father, we had wandered far from You, but through Your Son, You have brought us back. You gave Him up to death so that we might turn again to You and find our way to one another.

HIS POWER IS AMONG US

Therefore, we celebrate the reconciliation Christ has gained for us.

We ask You to sanctify these gifts by the power of Your Spirit, as we now fulfill your Son's command.

While He was at supper on the night He died for us, He took bread in His hands, and gave You thanks and praise. He broke the bread, gave it to His Disciples, and said: "Take this, all of you, and eat it, this is my Body which will be given up for you. At the end of the meal He took the cup. Again He praised you for Your goodness, gave the cup to His Disciples and said: "Take this, all of you, and drink from it: This is the Cup of my Blood, the Blood of the new and everlasting covenant. It will be shed for you and for all so that sins may be forgiven. Do this in memory of me."

Let us proclaim the mystery of faith

All: Lord by Your cross and resurrection You have set us free. You are the Savior of the world.

Priest: Father, calling to mind the death Your Son endured for our salvation, His glorious resurrection and ascension into heaven and ready to greet Him when He comes again, we offer You in thanksgiving this holy and living sacrifice.

Look with favor on Your Church's offering and see the Victim whose death has reconciled us to Yourself.

142

Grant that we, who are nourished by His body and Blood, may be filled with His Holy Spirit, and become one body, one spirit in Christ.

May He make us an everlasting gift to You and enable us to share in the inheritance of Your saints, with Mary, the Virgin Mother of God, with the Apostles, the Martyrs, and all Your Saints on whose constant intercession we rely for help.

Lord our God, Your Son has entrusted to us this pledge of His love. We celebrate the memory of His death and resurrection and bring You the gift You have given us, the sacrifice of reconciliation. Therefore, we ask You, Father, to accept us, together with Your Son.

Fill us with His Spirit through our sharing in this meal. May He take away all that divides us.

Lord, may this sacrifice, which has made our peace with You, advance the peace and salvation of all the world, strengthen, in faith and love Your pilgrim Church on earth; Your servant, Pope John Paul, our bishop ( ), and all the bishops, with the clergy and the entire people Your Son has gained for You. Father, hear the prayers of the families You have gathered here before You.

In mercy and love unite all Your children wherever they may be. Remember the deceased members of our families:

(Here we call out our family name:)

Remember especially all the miscarried, aborted and stillborn children and those who have never been consecrated to You.

Remember, too, those whose death came through violence. We give these souls to You in the name of our families and ask that they be welcomed into the Kingdom to be in Your presence with all the angels and saints in heaven.

In baptism they died with Christ; may they also share His resurrection, when Christ will raise our mortal bodies and make them like His own glory. Welcome into Your Kingdom our departed brothers and sisters and all who have left this world in Your friendship.

There we hope to share in Your glory when every tear will be wiped away. On that day we shall see You, our God, as You are. We shall become like You and see ourselves as You see us and praise You forever through Christ our Lord, from Whom all good things come.

Through Him, with Him, in Him, in the unity of the Holy Spirit, all glory and honor is Yours, Almighty Father, forever and ever.

All: AMEN.

Lord's Prayer:

Leader: To prepare for the Paschal meal, to welcome the Lord, we pray for forgiveness and unconditional love for ourselves and for our family members. Before we eat Christ's Body and drink His Blood, we must be one with Him and with all our brothers and sisters, especially those with whom we share the same body and blood lines.

Priest: **Let us ask our Father to forgive our sins and to bring us to forgive those who sin against us:**

All: Our Father, who art in Heaven
hallowed be thy name;
Thy kingdom come;
Thy will be done, on earth as it is in heaven.
Give us this day our daily bread;
and forgive us our trespasses, as we forgive
those who trespass against us,
and lead us not into temptation,
but deliver us from evil

Priest: **Deliver us, Lord, from every evil, and grant us peace in our day. In Your mercy keep us free from sin and protect us from all undue anxiety, as we wait in joyful hope for the coming of our Savior, Jesus Christ.**

All: For the Kingdom, the Power, and the Glory are Yours, now and forever. **AMEN.**

SIGN OF PEACE

Lord, Jesus Christ, You said to Your Apostles: "I leave you peace, my peace I give you." Look not on our sins, but on the faith of Your Church, and grant us the peace and unity of Your Kingdom where You live forever and ever. AMEN

Priest: The peace of the Lord be with you always.
All: And also with you.
Priest: Let us offer each other the sign of peace.

BREAKING OF THE BREAD

Lamb of God, You take away the sins of the world, have mercy on us. Lamb of God, You take away the sins of the world, have mercy on us. Lamb of God You take away the sins of the world, grant us peace.

May the mingling of the Body and Blood of our Lord Jesus Christ bring eternal life to us who receive it.

Priest: **Lord Jesus Christ, with faith in Your love and mercy, we eat Your Body and drink Your Blood. Let it not bring us or anyone in our family condemnation, but health in mind and body.**

As you go forward to receive Communion, let the deceased go with you. You might imagine him or her standing by your side, or if the deceased is a child, you might carry it in your arms. As you receive Communion, ask Jesus to fill you with His mercy and healing love in those parts of your being which still miss the deceased person or still feel wounded by that person. As you drink of the cup, let Jesus' precious Blood heal all the hurts that may block you from receiving the fullness of Jesus' life.

Reception of Communion

Prayer after Communion
(to be said by all)

May the love of God our Creator bless us. May Jesus be our Lord, our Savior and our Good Shepherd. Holy Spirit, fill us with Your graces and gifts. Come, Holy Spirit, direct our bodies, minds, hearts and souls to You. Come, God of Timelessness! Come, Giver of God's healing! Come, Light of Our Hearts Visit our souls. In Your gracious visit, bring us consolation and relief in our family sicknesses, our family suffering, our family fears and turmoils. In life's temptations fill us with Your divine power and mercy. In family sorrows, fill us with hope and peace. In all our family problems, be with us as our advocate. Come, Holy Spirit, we need You. Without You and Your divine help, we can do nothing good, and everything in our life is sinful. Fill our minds with Your peace and joy. Give us new hearts, filled with divine love. Let our hearts be Your fountain to bring this living water of divine love and mercy to thirsting souls in our family.

Give us a new spirit. Breathe on us Your Spirit of wisdom, understanding, fortitude, knowledge, counsel, piety and fear of the Lord.

Holy Spirit, let the gifts of our family become active and dynamic in all its members. Grant us those special gifts Your wisdom knows are best suited to our talents and personalities. Through those gifts, use us to build God's Kingdom.

Holy Spirit, grant us a spirit of love, joy and peace. Give us an attitude of kindness, goodness, gentleness toward our brothers, sisters, parents and all our relatives. Impart to us a spirit of self-control so that all we do or say may be directed to the glory of the Heavenly Father.

Holy Spirit, grant us and our family Your gift of healing. May this healing bring our family wholeness in body, mind and soul and make us Your instruments to bring healing to others by our prayers.

Holy Spirit, grant our family the greatest of all healings, the grace of eternal life. It was You Who entered into the tomb of Jesus on the First Easter. It was Your Divine Power that brought Jesus back to His glorious resurrection. Let us share in the resurrection victory of Jesus. Let us share in His victory over sickness, sin, death, every evil and every power of the devil now and eternally. Let each of us here be a channel of grace for these gifts to each member of our family.

Mary, Mother of Jesus and our Mother, pray with us. Pray that we and the other members of our family may experience a new Pentecost in our own lives, in the Church and throughout the world.

May we go forth as instruments of the Holy Spirit, filled with divine wisdom and power to bring God's love and healing to all members of our family, those present to us now, those of our ancestral past and those of our future generations. Pray for us, Mary, that, like you, we may be God's instruments to bring His peace and healing. Be to us always a Loving Mother of Perpetual Help. AMEN

When you are ready to give life as Jesus does, then see His Most Precious Blood flow from you to the deceased persons, healing all hurts, sinful patterns and occult bondages. Jesus, let Your Most Precious Blood flow back through these family lines to all those living or dead who need Your life, Your mercy and Your love.

PRAYER AFTER COMMUNION

All powerful God, by the power of this sacrament, give our brothers and sisters eternal happiness in the fellowship of the just. Release them from all bondages which have separated them from Your presence. Give them eternal happiness. We ask this through Christ our Lord.

PRAYER TO THE VIRGIN MARY

Mary, Holy Virgin Mother, we have received your Son, Jesus Christ. With love, you became His mother, gave birth to Him, nursed Him and helped Him grow to manhood. With love, we return Him to you, to hold once more, to love with all your heart.

Mother, ask God to forgive our sins and help us serve Him more faithfully. Keep us true to Christ until death, and let us come to praise Him with you forever and ever. AMEN

FINAL BLESSING

In His great love, the God of all consolation gave us the gift of life. May God bless us with faith in the resurrection of Jesus and with the hope of rising to new life. AMEN

To us who are alive, may He grant forgiveness, and to all who have died, a place of light and peace.

As we believe that Jesus rose from the dead, so may we live with Him forever in joy. AMEN

May Almighty God bless us, Father, Son and Holy Spirit. AMEN

HEALING OF ANCESTRY

A Prayer of Deliverance

Eternal Father,

As a community of faith and a family in prayer, we gather to give you praise, adoration and thanksgiving in all things. We pray for all the deceased members of the families represented here, and all those who, in the past, were born deceased still-born, miscarried, aborted, never committed to God and those who died an early death. We pray for the family members who died brutally or violently, lost in the war or otherwise died from strange and mysterious illnesses, from great fears, acts of cowardice, sudden death, in mysterious fires and for all who were rejected by the family, wanderers and lost members, adopted, abandoned, or rejected.

We pray for all the members of the families represented here who were addicted to drugs, alcohol, games, compulsions of all kinds, gambling, lust, deceitfulness, addictive shopping, and for family members unduly attached to values of the world, money, prestige, power and control over persons or things.

We pray for those who died and were never prayed for and those buried without a proper funeral. We pray for those who died by their own hand and for those who were murderers or accomplices. We pray for those who died through suffocation or were abandoned, for those afflicted with great phobias, emotional instability, insanity, unexplained illness and from all other causes known by God alone.

We ask release from all bondage coming from the occult, under any form practiced by family members in the past or in the present affecting living members in whatever negative form of bondage, infirmity, emotional or physical illness, addictions of any kind, spiritual torment or other confusion. I hereby rebuke and cast out in the Name of Jesus Christ, from all living members of these families, the following dark and binding forces of spiritual and emotional torment, undue anxieties, tensions and stress, violence, prejudice, error, devaluation, self-hatred, retaliation, arrogance and deceitful pride in all its forms.

We ask deliverance from fears of all kinds — the fear of being found out, the fear of ghosts, fears of natural elements such as heights, thunder, lightning, wind, water, fire, closed spaces, fearful dreams, the fear of rejection, the fear of intimacy, the fear of failure, the fear of success, the fear of man, the fear of woman, the fear of darkness and all other kinds of fears, spiritual, emotional or physical from whatever source.

I hereby rebuke and cast out, in the Name of Jesus Christ all dark and binding forces of superstition, slander, destructive lies and falsehoods, deception in all its forms and attempts to destroy others' reputation, lust, homosexuality, lesbianism, incest and perversions of all kinds. I hereby rebuke and cast out, in the Name of Jesus Christ obsessive and compulsive destructive behavior, manic attitudes, depressions, denial and deceitful games, abandonment, rage, excessive anger, guilt, vengeance and self-destructive anxieties, attitudes and attempts.

I hereby rebuke and cast out, in the Name of Jesus Christ, the following dark and binding forces called confusion, chaos, rebellion, arrogance, hallucinations, sleep walking, addictions, fortune telling in all its forms, witchcraft, satanism, necromancy, santeria, black mass, and occultism in all its forms.

In the Name of Jesus Christ, I rebuke and cast out all deceitful and destructive forces of despair, betrayal, uncontrolled frustrations, bitterness, despondency, repression, projection in all its forms, manipulation and control, the fear of rejection, self-deceit, rejection and self-rejection, exaggerated anxieties, withdrawal, self-pity, false guilt and perversions of all kinds.

I rebuke and cast out in the Name of Jesus Christ, the dark and binding forces of pride, denial, fantasies, doubt, mockery, repression, hopelessness, fear of insanity, fear of perdition, infidelity, abuses of all kinds, verbal, mental, emotional, physical, or spiritual. I rebuke and cast out in the Name of Jesus Christ all false gods and idols.

151

Seal, I break you in the Name of Jesus Christ
Seal, I break you in the Name of Jesus Christ
Seal, I break you in the Name of Jesus Christ

I hearby break and cast out in the Name of Jesus Christ all curses of any kind placed upon the members of the families represented here and all ancestry of these families.

I hearby break and sever by the power of the Word of God and the Sword of the Spirit all negative ancestral spirits and influences of any kind from whatever source, genetic, spiritual, physical, emotional or psychic affecting the living members of these families wherever they may now be living.

In the name of all these past and lost or injured souls, I ask forgiveness for those who died unforgiven and unforgiving. For them, we ask deliverance from present darkness, confusion and chaos. As a family, we raise up to God all the ancestors who were never baptized for whatever reason. We ask the Lord to accept them, through the baptism of desire, into the family of the Church with a right to Heaven. We bestow upon each one of them the name of family members who surrounded them at the time of their death. We command the Holy Angels, in the Name of Jesus Christ, to lead all these souls into Paradise to be forever in the Presence of our heavenly Father, the angels, and the saints and from this moment on, to be intercessors for all the living members of the families represented here today. I claim the most Precious Blood of Jesus Christ upon all members of these families, that they be protected form all harm, injury, accident, illness and the wiles of the devil. I also ask the Holy Angels to be, now and always, sentries of protection for all the members of the families represented here today. I ask the angels to protect their possessions from all harm and destructive forces.

We make our prayer in the Name of Jesus of Nazareth who's compassionate love heals all wounds through forgiveness, mercy and prayer. AMEN.

AFTERWORD

Partners In Healing:
Immaculate Heart of Mary/Reconciliation at La Salette
Sacred Heart of Jesus/Divine Mercy

Let us now, in this the "Afterword," return to the image which opened the "Foreword" to this book. It was the apparition of Our Lady, in the posture of bent grief. She was weeping for all her children, — in front of those two shepherd children — on that mountaintop in La Salette, France on September 19, 1846.

Yet in all the readings of the Gospel, there is not one reference to Our Blessed Mother weeping. But her tears rained down at La Salette, and surely this sorrowing Mother must have wept at the foot of the Cross. Indeed, on an anguished journey, she followed His bloodied footsteps there. She was witness to the Cross; she was part of the experience of her Son dying for all humanity.

This same strong woman returned to earth at La Salette to warn humanity that if they failed to observe the commandments of God and the laws of the Church, she could not continue to hold back the arm of her Son from striking the unfaithful children of God. Her heart was heavy because His children were not listening.

However, remember her message held light, as well as darkness. She also bore the Good News of reconciliation. She bore witness to the Divine Mercy of The Sacred Heart of Jesus.

This mixed message of doom and hope was represented by the cross which Our Lady wore around her neck when she appeared at La Salette. On one side above the outstretched arm of Jesus was a hammer — a symbolic reminder that each time we sin we drive the nails deeper into the hands of the suffering Jesus. On the other side were the pliers — a symbolic reminder that through repentance and reconciliation and conversion of our hearts, we take those nails from the hands of the suffering Jesus.

Our Lady of La Salette is reconciler of all sinners, now and at the end of our days. Her message, like the message of all authenticated apparitions of Our Blessed Mother, is "Come back to The Cross." The experience of the Cross is loneliness, darkness and abandonment. The experience of the Cross is also purification through suffering, which leads to spiritual sunshine, joy and resurrection.

We need to ask Mary to keep us near her Immaculate Heart, for it is that heart which opens up that gentle path which leads to the Sacred Heart of her Son, and His Divine Mercy. Remember, the Lord gave Mary to us as our mother. She will guide us there, to the Sacred Heart of her Son, where we will experience His Divine Mercy, if only we ask.

Sister Faustina and The Image of Divine Mercy

In the 1930's, over the course of successive years, Jesus appeared to Sister Faustina Kowalska, who had entered the Congregation of the Sisters of Our Lady of Mercy in Poland in 1925. Sister Faustina, who died in 1938, (and was beatified on Divine Mercy Sunday, 1993) was instructed by Jesus to initiate a devotion in the form of a chaplet of Divine Mercy, teaching the following prayer to be said on the beads of the Rosary:

"First you will say one OUR FATHER AND HAIL MARY and the I BELIEVE IN GOD. Then on the OUR FATHER beads you will say the following words: 'Eternal Father, I offer you the Body and Blood, Soul and Divinity of Your dearly beloved Son, Our Lord Jesus Christ, in atonement for our sins and those of the whole world.' On the HAIL MARY beads you will say the following words: 'For the sake of His sorrowful Passion have mercy on us and on the whole world.' In conclusion, three times you will recite these words: 'Holy God, Holy Mighty One, Holy Immortal One, have mercy on us and on the whole world.'"[1]

Sister Faustina was also told by Jesus of the graces that would come from the recitation of the chaplet:

"Oh what great graces I will grant to souls who say this chaplet; the very depths of My tender mercy are stirred for the sake of those who say the chaplet. Write down these words, My daughter. Speak to the world about My mercy; let all mankind recognize My unfathomable mercy. It is a sign for end times; after it will come the day of justice. While there is still time, let them have recourse to the fount of My mercy; let them profit from the Blood and Water which gushed forth from them."[2]

Jesus asked Sister Faustina to have a painting made in the Image of His Divine Mercy. He described what He wanted depicted: red and white rays flowing from His wounded heart offering Divine Mercy, the red and white symbolizing the blood and water which flowed as His heart was pierced on the Cross. Jesus told her that whoever venerated this Image, whoever took time at the hour of three to contemplate, meditate on His Passion, would receive through the merits of that Passion whatever they asked for at the moment of death.

Theologians who have been studying this devotion to the Divine Mercy now see it as a fulfillment of the devotion to the Sacred Heart of Jesus, for His mercy flows from His Sacred Heart.

For many years the devotion to the Image of Divine Mercy was suppressed because of the misinterpretation of the writings of Sister Faustina. But shortly following her death, a young Polish seminarian was introduced to her life and works. He would frequently pray at her tomb in Cracow. That seminarian later became bishop of Cracow, and he led the cause for beatification of Sister Faustina. He later was elevated to the Chair of St. Peter, and he is our Holy Father Pope John Paul II."

The first image of The Divine Mercy was painted in 1934 in Vilnius by E. Kazimierowski, under Sister Faustina's guidance. Another was painted in 1957 by Adam Styka, and this is in the Sanctuary of The Divine Mercy at the Congregation of Marian Helpers in Stockbridge, Mass. The latest version was painted by Robert O. Skemp in 1982.[3]

Conclusion

In all depictions of the Image, multiple rays shine forth from the Sacred Heart, from the Divine Heart of Jesus. Each one can be thought to signify a gift, a gift that we need: the gift of generosity; the gift of forgiveness, the gift of repentance, the gift of gentleness; the gift of tears; the gift of discovery that we are sons and daughters of our Father in heaven, created in His likeness and goodness.

We need to bring the image of Divine Mercy into our homes and into our hearts, and our weeping Mother beckons us to do so. Each time we contemplate the image, we must consider how we have used that hammer to nail Jesus to the Cross. We must also change our hearts and use the pliers. The sorrowing Immaculate Heart of Mary summons us to conversion. As Reconciler she bears the Good News that through penance, prayer and sacrifice we witness to total love of God through Jesus to the Father in Heaven.

In such a way are we healed. In such a way do we become healers.

——Father Albert A. Fredette, M. S.,
March 19, 1993

END NOTES

Foreword

1. Jean Jaouen, M.S., *A Grace Called La Salette, A Story for the World*, as translated by Normand Theroux, M. S. (Attleboro, Massachusetts: La Salette Publications, 1991), p. 339.

Introduction

1. Nassif J. Cannon Jr., M.D., "Broken Healers — Physicians and Priests," *The Priest*, September, 1988.

The Story of La Salette Briefly Told

1. Donald Paradis, M.S., *The Missionaries of La Salette: From France to North America* (Attleboro, Massachusetts: La Salette Publications, 1992), back cover page.

2. *Ibid.*, p. 11.

Chapter III

1. Dr. Kenneth McAll, *Healing the Family Tree* (London: Sheldon Press, 1982), p. 56.

2. *Ibid.*, p. 58.

Afterword

1. Sister M. Faustina Kowalska, *Divine Mercy in My Soul, The Diary of the Servant of God*_(Stockbridge, Mass.: Marian Press, 1987), p. 208.

2. *Ibid.*, p. 332.

3. *Ibid.*, picture pages.

HIS POWER IS AMONG US

Rev. Albert A. Fredette holds a doctor of ministry degree with concentration in counseling from Andover-Newton School of Theology, a master's in missiology-community development from St. Paul University, Ottawa, Canada, and a master of theology degree from La Salette Seminary, Attleboro, Mass., where he was ordained in 1952. He has served as director of the pastoral care department, director of clinical pastoral education and coordinator of healing ministries at St. Vincent Medical Center in Toledo, Ohio. Fr. Fredette continues to practice his healing ministry extensively in this country, and the Philippines through conferences, workshops, Masses and special services. He has published on the topic of pastoral counseling and produced professional audio cassettes on counseling and the healing ministry. He has also conducted numerous seminars and conferences on these topics.

Patricia A. Kelly, an associate professor of journalism at Northeastern University's School of Journalism, Boston, Mass., has a master's degree and a Ph.D. in English from Brown University. She has 12 years experience teaching writing, reporting and literature at the university level. She has worked as a reporter and editor for four Massachusetts daily newspapers and holds first place awards from United Press International, New England Press Association, and the Massachusetts Press Association for her writing and reporting. Her academic publications include: *Police and the Media: Bridging Troubled Waters* (Charles C. Thomas, Publishers, 1987); "Police and the Media: The Problem," (a nationally-circulated white paper published by Gannett Foundation and National Press Photographers Association, 1990), and "The Media and the Police: Contemporary Experiments in Cross-Education," in *New Perspectives in Policing* (Autumn House, 1992).

HIS POWER IS AMONG US